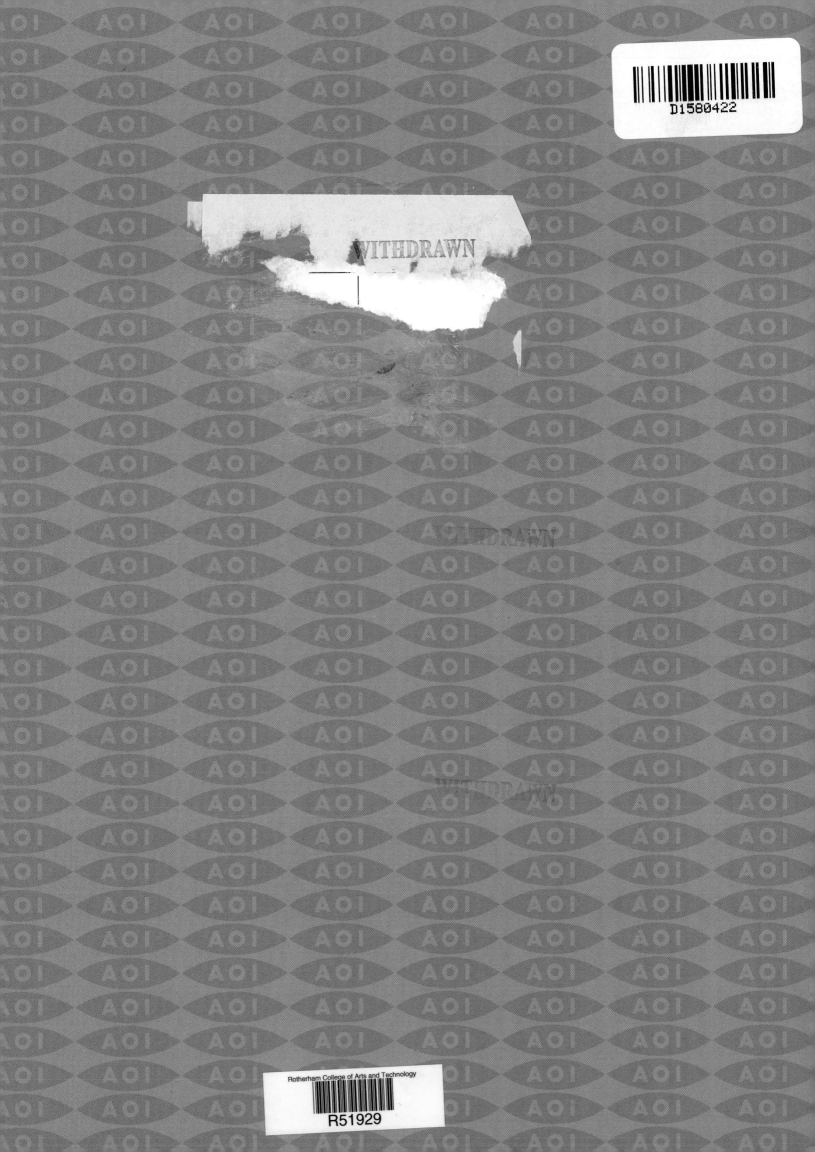

Images 29

Images **29**

The only jury-selected illustration annual in the UK, Images presents an overview of the wealth and variety of work produced in the UK today. Now with a new, further improved design concept, it provides commissioners with easy access to established illustrators and emerging new talents.
An indispensable tool for leading industry professionals, this catalogue of illustration excellence is an essential publication for academics, students and practitioners alike.

Acknowledgements
We are grateful for the support of the many organisations and individuals who contribute to the success of the Images exhibition and annual by submitting their best work to be judged by their peers.

Our dedicated team of judges for applying their expertise to the difficult task of selecting this year's work.

Simon Sharville for his creative impact and diplomacy during the design process.

Nicole Peli for her usual effectiveness and healthy pragmatism during the production of Images 29.

Geoff Grandfield for the use of his illustration 'Travel Cliff' on the cover.

Daryl Waller for the use of his illustration 'Tom Violence' on the Images 30 Call for Entries form.

Stuart Briers for his ongoing support (IT and anything else) and patience when faced with yet another question about the correct use of the AOI database.

Robert Lands, Lawyer at Finers Stephens Innocent, not only for his legal advice but also for his constant interest in the development of the organisation.

All our dedicated casual staff and volunteers for their invaluable assistance with the competition and exhibition, in particular: Stephanie Alexander, Sabine Reimer, Delphine Lebourgeois, Abigail Conway, Michelle Lewarton-Smith, Anna Pidgeon.

1

Images 29 edited and published by
The Association of Illustrators
2nd Floor, Back Building
150 Curtain Road
London
EC2A 3AR

Tel. +44 (0)20 7613 4328
Fax +44 (0)20 7613 4417
email: info@theaoi.com
www.theAOI.com

Production in China by
Hong Kong Graphics and Printing Ltd
Tel: (852) 2976 0289
Fax: (852) 2976 0292

The Association of Illustrators
AOI Volunteer Council of Management:
Paul Bowman, Russell Cobb, Adam Graff, Rod Hunt, Alison Lang, Simon Pemberton, Michael Sheehy, Louise Weir

AOI Chair: Michael Bramman

AOI Images Committee:
Silvia Baumgart, Michael Bramman, Russell Cobb, Adam Graff, Alison Lang

Advisors: Stuart Briers, Frazer Hudson, Robert Lands, Simon Stern, Fig Taylor, Ruth Gladwin, Stephanie Alexander, Alison Branaghan, Elliot Haag, Chris Haughton, Tony Healey, Christine Jopling, Samantha Lewis, Jimmy Turrell, Adrian Valencia, Bee Willey, Jo Young

Manager: Silvia Baumgart
silvia@theaoi.com

Exhibitions and Events Co-ordinator: Stella Di Meo
events@theaoi.com

Publications/Membership Co-ordinator: Derek Brazell
info@theaoi.com

Membership Co-ordinator/Administrative Assistant:
Anna Hallam
info@theaoi.com

Book Design: Simon Sharville, London
www.simonsharville.co.uk

Contents

About the **Association of Illustrators**

The Association of Illustrators was established in 1973 to advance and protect illustrators' rights and to encourage professional standards. It is a non-profit making trade association and members consist primarily of freelance illustrators as well as agents, clients, students and lecturers. As the only body to represent illustrators and campaign for their rights in the UK, the AOI has successfully increased the standing of illustration as a profession and improved the commercial and ethical conditions of employment for illustrators.

The AOI provides a voice for professional illustrators and by force of numbers and expertise is able to enforce the rights of freelance illustrators at every stage of their careers. The AOI is run by a Manager who executes the policies and objectives of a volunteer Council of Management supported by administrative staff.

Campaigning and Net-working

The AOI is responsible for establishing the right for illustrators to retain ownership of their artwork and helped to establish the secondary rights arm of the Designers and Artists Copyright Society (DACS), the UK visual arts collecting society. In addition, it is a member of the Creators Rights Alliance (CRA), the British Copyright Council (BCC), and a founder member of the European Illustrators Forum (EIF).

Retaining of Artwork
Each commission, while serving the needs of the brief, generates an original. Its lifetime in print will contribute to the world's greatest, most accessible and diverse wall-less art gallery. Therefore, it is important that the artist is aware of the value of the original and should always retain ownership of the original artwork. The AOI sells stickers ensuring that artwork is returned to the illustrator.

Design and Artists Copyright Society (DACS)
DACS is a not-for-profit membership based organisation representing various creators, including illustrators. They provide a range of licencing services for copyright consumers seeking to licence the individual rights of an artist. Licences for secondary uses of artistic works such as photocopying and television use are administered under collective licencing schemes on behalf of all visual creators. DACS negotiates a share of revenue from these schemes and distributes payments through their Payback service.
DACS has been distributing this revenue since 1999, and has seen massive growth in licencing revenue pay-outs and in the numbers of visual creators benefiting since then.
The AOI helped to establish the secondary rights arm of DACS and our patron Simon Stern sits on their board. AOI also distributes the DACS application form to members each year.

Creators Rights Alliance (CRA)
CRA was formed in 2001 and is now a group of seventeen organisations, comprising approximately 120,000 individual copyright creators and content providers working throughout the UK media marketplace.
The CRA consists of such organisations as the Musicians Union, the National Union of Journalists, the Association of Photographers, Equity and the Society of Authors amongst others, as well as the AOI.
The aim of the Alliance is to defend its members' interests against abuses of creators' rights in all media, including

magazine and newspaper publishing and broadcasting. The problems that we all face as illustrators are shared across a whole range of creative industries. The lack of equality between individual sole trader, freelance creators, and huge publishing multinationals complete with teams of lawyers has never been more apparent.
These two parties are seen as equally equipped to negotiate with one another under the eyes of the law but recent events have shown that the playing field is anything but level.
As a part of the CRA the AOI can, on behalf of its members, attempt matters that its limited resources would make it difficult or impossible to achieve alone. The AOI is now able to lobby parliament for changes in the law, aligning UK law more closely with those of our European neighbours, who are widely seen as more creator friendly. We are also, as part of the CRA, commissioning further research into the extent of creators' rights abuses, with a view to challenging the Dept. of Trade and Industry, and looking at the shortcomings of the new communications bill from a creator's perspective.

European Illustrators Forum (EIF)
Founded in 2003, the European Illustrators Forum now has 16 member associations in Europe. Its aim is to lobby the European Parliament for better legislation for creative people and create awareness of illustration in the wider public on an international level and reach illustrators that are not yet associated with trade organisations.
Through joint ventures, members can for example tour exhibitions Europe wide or organise high profile conferences funded by the European Union. It is important for each association to be part of a wider network to gain more political force and greater recognition of issues related to illustration. The EIF is currently working on a basic licence agreement valid throughout the European Union.

Information and Support Services

Portfolio Advice
Members are entitled to more than 50% discount on a one-hour consultation with the AOI's portfolio consultant. Objective advice is given on portfolio presentation, content and suitable illustration markets and agents.

THE JOURNAL
The Association of Illustrators' (AOI) Journal covers a wide range of issues related to the illustration industry including:
• current industry affairs
• illustration
• events
• reviews
• interviews
• letters
Regular contributors include practitioners, educators and industry professionals. The Journal provides a forum for on-going debate and a valuable insight into contemporary illustration. Published six times a year. Free to members.
The Journal is available to non-members on subscription.

Professional Advice
Members have access to a special trained member of staff if they need advice about pricing commissions, copyright and ethics problems.

Publications
The AOI publishes several guides to professional practice, including *Survive* and *Rights*, and client directories, which are updated every year and hold in total more than 700 contact details. The client directories not only publish details of commissioners of illustration in advertising, editorial and publishing but also include useful information on what styles are preferred by an agency, magazine, children's book publisher etc. New to the list is the *Report on Illustration Fees and Standards of Pricing* published in February 2005, compiling results of a survey the AOI has conducted into pricing structures and rates throughout the industry.

Business Advice
Members are entitled to a free consultation with the AOI Chartered Accountant who can advise on accounting, National Insurance, tax, VAT and book-keeping.

Discounts
Members receive large discounts on AOI events, publications and many art material suppliers nationwide.

Legal Advice
Full and Associate members receive bespoke advice on ethics and contractual problems, copyright and moral right disputes.

Return of Artwork Stickers
Available to AOI members only. These stickers help safeguard the return of artwork.

Students and Newly Professional Illustrators
Our seminars and publications combined with the many services we offer provide practical support to illustrators in the early stages of their career.

Events
The AOI runs an annual programme of events, which include one-day conferences, evening lectures, themed exhibitions and illustration projects. These include talks by leading illustrators as well as representatives from all areas of the illustration field, and cover such subjects as children's book illustration, aspects of professional practice, new technologies and illustrators' agents. AOI members are entitled to discounted tickets.

Membership
To request further information or a membership application form, please telephone +44 (0)20 7613 4328

Website
Visit the AOI's website at www.theAOI.com for details of the Association's activities, including samples from current and past Journals, details of forthcoming events and online tickets, the AOI's history, and to order publications and display online portfolios.

4

Foreword by **Michael Bramman**

'The surprise of the summer', this was the verdict of one of the critics on the Radio 4 Arts Review programme which reported on the Images 28 exhibition held at the Mall Galleries last year.

Public awareness and the profile of illustration has increased dramatically over the last two years. There has been an explosion of publications using and celebrating illustration, and the profession is, at last, getting the critical recognition it deserves. This shift in attitudes is reflected by the 25% increase in the number of entries for the Images 29 competition compared to the previous year.

During the exchanges between the forum of critics on the programme it was evident that there was a need to address the issue of the context of the work shown. In this year's exhibition we will be showing examples of the printed matter alongside the original artwork for the commission. This should explain blank or empty areas in some illustrations where the designer usually sets typography. A more explanatory approach to the exhibition will contribute to the visitors' understanding of the illustrator's working process and raise the public's awareness of illustration. To clarify another point of confusion as to whether or not the unpublished section represents rejected work, it is common illustration practice for artists to produce self-promotional, experimental and authorial work which has the potential for use by clients at a future date. In this section we feature the best of this work.

The AOI is committed to promoting exhibitions and events which are of interest to the public and encourage a greater understanding and appreciation of illustration.

I have also proposed to the Council that the AOI develops an online illustration archive. This archive will document the history of illustration along with all aspects of illustration practice from cave art to digital work. This will act as a research tool and designed to be educational, informative and entertaining.

At this year's exhibition we are again offering The Critic's Award to be selected from the work in the annual by Tom Lubbock, art critic of The Independent, and presented by him at the private view. Andrzej Klimowski will present the AOI's Gold, Silver and Bronze Awards for the seven categories.

We have taken literally the expression, 'Everyone's a critic', and will be inviting a wide spectrum of practitioners of the arts and cultural commentators to choose and present the Critic's Award in future exhibitions.

Our thanks to all the international group of judges involved, many of them have supported the AOI over the years.

With the new presentation of the work and the high standard of the illustration published I hope you will be as pleased to own a copy of Images as we have been to publish it.

Michael Bramman
AOI Chair

Introduction **Andrzej Klimowski**

All things being well, an illustrator is kept busy working for commercial clients and has little time to theorise about the nature of his or her discipline. It is through the practice of making graphic works that the illustrator discovers new ideas and develops an individual language. However, like most professions, illustration is affected by the fluctuations of a free market economy and is sometimes left on the margins. In the 1980's, there was almost too much of it whilst throughout much of the following decade it seemed to have faded as a discipline.

It is exactly in times of difficulty that one is drawn to reflect on the nature of one's profession and on how to evolve as an artist. When commissions are lacking, illustrators have to create a market for their work. Here they are no different to fine artists who in one way or another have to impose their presence onto the public. There are many mechanisms designed to facilitate this difficult, often arduous task: galleries, agents, publications (such as this one) and the press exist for this very purpose. Not everyone can persuade a gallery or an agent to represent them, let alone hope to be promoted in books or by the press. So what should an illustrator do?

Perhaps we should ask an even more basic question. Why should we pursue such a volatile profession in the first place? In my own case, the answer is simple: I have been working at it for thirty years and it is too late to do anything else. Yet the nature of my work has changed. I no longer receive a steady flow of commissions for book cover

illustrations which used to keep me busy for so many years. I illustrate my own books, publish prints and teach, and it is as a teacher that I wish to pursue this reflection further.

I think I have learnt a lot through the exchange of ideas and philosophies with my colleagues and my students. I am aware that illustration is just one ingredient in the very broad field of visual communication. When, at the Royal College of Art, Professor Dan Fern merged the illustration and graphic design departments into the one department of Communication Art and Design it was considered a daring, even rash move. Yet it was perfectly logical in the way that it mirrored the realities of the commercial world. An illustrator needs to have a knowledge of design in order to survive. Graphic images and illustrations are created as much for the screen and for architectural spaces as they are for print. Thus the young illustration student picks up a knowledge of film grammar and typography by sitting in on critiques and seminars primarily aimed at his design and multimedia peers.

After graduating, many of our students share studio space or form small, independent design groups. Thus they are able to continue their critical debates together. These design groups are not short of illustrators (Abake and Thomas/Mathews). Illustration injects life into much of graphic design. It has vitality, playfulness and lends projects an individual touch. Graphic design is often identified as a discipline which is fundamentally concerned with solving problems. It has to convey a

client's message in the most succinct way possible. Often the message needs to be direct, free of all ambiguity. If a road sign should be ambiguous and open to interpretation we would be in serious trouble. However, not all clients' messages need to be as direct as a road sign. Sometimes the subject which is being communicated is subliminal or oblique. Take for example the book cover for a novel. The designer cannot afford to be literal or else he risks destroying the reader's imagination. Working with an illustrator who can emphathize with the book's atmosphere or mood can elevate the cover to a poetic statement. What an illustrator can share with a novelist is having an individual voice which implies an original style.

Style of course is a major preoccupation with illustrators. On the one hand, an illustrator strives to develop an individual style in order to be recognized and be distinguished from other illustrators. He or she can thus be cast by an art director, agent or designer for the right or most appropriate commissions. On the other hand, style can lead to a set of mannerisms which can type cast illustrators, limiting their scope and hindering them from further developing as artists. It is not difficult to identify the illustrators who have become enslaved by their own style.

Equally, one can understand what motivates them to continue working along one line which has bought them peer acclaim and a measure of financial security. What they have lost however is far more precious. They have lost the vitality of their earlier work;

6

something which was once risky, innovative and bold has become a formula. We need to reinvent ourselves, not just for the sake of it, but to remain fresh, curious, inquisitive and vital. What helps is to be continually working for oneself, that is to say to produce work other than for commercial use. Alongside illustrations for publication in books, magazines and the digital media an illustrator should be making experimental pieces as a personal investigation into form, structure, colour, technique etc.: art for art's sake. It may be exhibited or it may simply disappear into the plan chest. Sooner or later it will find its way into commissioned illustration, revitalised and new.

Two of my colleagues at the RCA, Anne Howeson and Debbie Cook, have been running drawing projects particularly aimed at illustration students. They invite students to approach the subject matter they are to draw from three points of view: from direct observation, the imagination and memory. If illustrators seriously take on board all three approaches as part of their practice then I think they are destined to succeed as artists. Our imagination is reinforced by an observing eye and a trained memory. We develop an understanding of the world by seeing the way things look, by observing the way people and animals behave. If our sketchbooks are filled with the vocabulary of body language or with everyday objects or nature observed from a variety of angles, we are sitting on an archive that can give credence to the fictional worlds that we are constructing from our imaginations. Memory provides us with clues to our own psychic

makeup, for memory is subjective and reveals our true personality.

You will have to look hard to find works of true originality in this book. Like all compendiums of specialised graphic disciplines we are inevitably confronted by the good, the bad and the ugly. The publication is holding up a mirror to the commercial world. This world is imperfect, often vulgar.

Look hard however and you will find examples that have the vitality that I have been referring to. We have to remember that illustrations live their natural life on the covers of books, on posters in the streets or among the columns of text in newspapers and magazines. Compressed together in one volume they remind me of passengers in fancy costumes in an overcrowded train.

Andrzej Klimowski,
Professor in Illustration, RCA, London

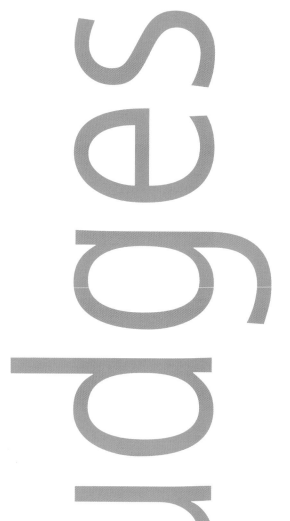

Advertising

Brian Cairns
Illustrator

Max Ellis
Illustrator

Carlton Hibbert
.net Magazine
Art Editor

Sophie Hinds
Saatchi & Saatchi
Art Buyer

Rian Hughes
Illustrator
Designer
Typographer

Design

Dylan Channon
Future Publishing
Senior Art Editor

Richard Krzyzak
CMP Information Ltd.
Group Art Director

Chris Wormell
Illustrator

New Media

Beach
Illustrator

Jim Chambers
Channel 4
Art Director/Graphic Designer

Chris Corr
Illustrator

Charles Hively
3x3 Magazine
Publisher/Design Director

Phill McVicar
Euro RSCG KLP
Senior Art Director

Graham Rolfe
Haymarket Publishing
Senior Designer

Crispian Brown
Caspian Publishing Ltd
Creative Director

Roger Browning
The Guardian
Head of Design

Andrew Foster
Illustrator &
Illustration Subject Leader
MA Communication Design
@ Central St.Martins
School of Art & Design

Chris Kasch
Illustrator

Alison Lawn
New Scientist
Art Director

Amanda Scope
Top Santé Magazine
Art Director

Anna Billson
Puffin Books
Art Director

Martin Colyer
Reader's Digest Magazine
Design Director

Lisa Kopper
Illustrator

Sarah McMenemy
Illustrator

Sarah Mears
Essex County Libraries
Culture and Adult Learning
Services Manager

Matt Bookman
Freelance Graphic
Designer/ Illustrator

Peter Dyer
Freelance Art Director

Geoff Grandfield
Illustrator

Jonny Hannah
Illustrator

Jamie Trendall
Radio Times
Deputy Art Editor

William Webb
Bloomsbury Publishing
Design Director

Greg Clarke
Illustrator

Ben Cox
CIA
Agent

Dan Fern
RCA
Head of Department,
Communication Art and Design
Royal College of Art

Willi Gray
Illustrator

Mike Litherland
Senior Lecturer BA Illustration
Westminster University

Simon Carbery
Copy Writer

Tony Chambers
Wallpaper*
Creative Director

Jonathan Cusick
Illustrator

Nick Hardcastle
Illustrator

Sue Vago
The Economist
Senior Designer

9

The **Critic's** Award

The Critic's Award was established in 2004 to add another perspective to the usual discussions amongst illustrators and industry professionals and their peers – in other words, the commercial world of illustration. Each year, personalities from the world of arts and culture are invited to choose their favourite piece of illustration from all works published in Images and write a short comment on their choice. The critic's view does not necessarily reflect the Association of Illustrators' policies or objectives but expresses the personal opinion of the critic. Tom Lubbock's comment is provocative, some might say missing the point, but it will certainly stir heated discussions. From the beginning, this has been the Critic's Award's intention: to open a debate on illustration not only to a wider public but also to illustrators and their clients.

AOI Council

Delphine Lebourgeois, 'What is a Sex Toy'
selected for the Critic's Award by Tom Lubbock

I found it disheartening, looking at the images in this book. They're most of them so bloody twee. There's a strain of whimsicalness, which seems to be default mode for the commercial illustrator. The blame, I'm sure, must be shared - between the artists themselves, the art-directors whose briefs they're following, and perhaps the judges who made this selection. But very quickly I found myself looking for something severe, laconic and clever, and hardly ever finding it.

It is normal for illustration and fine art to borrow vigorously from one another. But the art that's been dominant in the UK for the last fifteen years or so seems to have made little impact here. It has itself borrowed a good deal from illustration, or from adverts anyway - but the favour hasn't been returned. In Daryl Waller's work there are some useful echoes of Gary Hume, and of David Shrigley, but apart from that nothing. I would have thought

that the sangfroid and conceptual sharpness of the YBA's would be something an illustrator could very profitably learn from – plus A FEELING FOR a lateral relationship between image and meaning, or between image and text. The pictorial uses of text seemed especially feeble.

I half suspect that illustration has become a haven for visual artists who want to escape from what fine art has become. But whatever its limitations as art, this work is a source of strength that illustration should not neglect. So my vote is tactical. In the cause of the laconic and the lateral, and against the virtuosic, I nominate an image from the student category, called 'What is a Sex Toy'?, by Delphine Lebourgeois.

Tom Lubbock

Tom Lubbock started his career as an illustrator. He is currently an art critic for The Independent (where he also did the Saturday cartoon from 1999-2004). He writes for various publications on contemporary art and occasionally on illustration.

Delphine Lebourgeois studied Fine Art in Lyon in France for 3 years focusing mainly on photography.
During the last year of her BA, she travelled to Vietnam where she started to enjoy drawing as an honest and immediate way of expressing her ideas and feelings. She moved to London, had a daughter and, in January 2005, graduated with an MA in Communication Design from Central St Martins. Studying for an MA gave her the opportunity to pursue and develop her visual language. She chose parenthood as her MA project because it gave her many opportunities to be thought provoking and humorous. She has been largely inspired by her daughter, people around her as well as artists such as Steven Appleby.
She lives and works as a freelance illustrator in London.

advertising

Brian Cairns
Max Ellis
Carlton Hibbert
Sophie Hinds
Rian Hughes

Adrian Johnson

Adrian Johnson has been illustrating for the last seven years since graduating from Kingston University. During that time he has worked prolifically for a plethora of clients in the UK and abroad across editorial, advertising, children's books and animation fields. Amongst some of his clients have been Orange, Nissan, The Design Council, The Guardian, and Sky+, working with HHCL Red Cell and Studio AKA.

Gold

01 **Bear and Hunter**

Medium Mixed media

Brief To illustrate a series of press ads for Sky+ on the theme of odd couples.

Commissioned by Maria Deluca

Agency HHCL Red Cell

Client Sky +

In November 2003 he had his first major exhibition 'A Lovely Pair' with fellow illustrator McFaul at the Coningsby Gallery, London. Since 'A Lovely Pair' he became one of the founding members of the art and illustration collective, Black Convoy, exhibiting at the 'Full English' show at The Apartment (New York) in February 2005.

Adrian works from his East London studio and teaches part-time on the illustration degree at Kingston University.

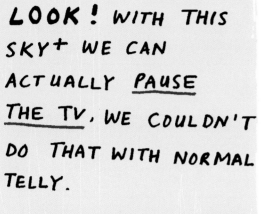

silver

Andy Smith

Andy Smith graduated from the RCA in 1998. His work is digital but derives from drawing and silkscreen printing and has been used in the fields of illustration, animation and design. His illustration has featured in numerous advertising campaigns, publishing and editorials, and he has animated and directed a commercial for Nike. Andy's client list includes Mercedes, Vauxhall, Expedia, London Transport, Oddbins, Orange, Vodaphone, Penguin Books, The Guardian, The Sunday Telegraph and The Independent and his work has won D&AD, Creative Circle and AOI awards. He has produced several self-published silkscreen printed books, which are available from his website www.asmithillustration.com, and various stockists in London.

He lives in East London.

02 **Stop Searching...**

Medium Digital

Brief Show the wide range of leisure activities available on holiday

Commissioned by Dave Wilsher

Agency C.H.I.

Client Expedia

Simon was born near Liverpool moving to London to study his degree at London College of Printing then a Masters in Illustration at Central St. Martins College of Art. He now lives and works in the East End of London with a Studio overlooking London Fields.

His work has always been fuelled by a fascination with texture, space and mark making that now expresses itself through painting, drawing and collaged "found elements" that are brought together in a digital environment.

Simon works extensively for a large U.K and USA client list across design, advertising, editorial and publishing fields. His work has featured in several contemporary illustration publications and he is a previous winner of an Images Bronze Award for Design and New Media. Simon's work has appeared in numerous exhibitions in the U.K and USA most recently in the 3x3 Contemporary Illustration Awards and exhibition in New York.

Travel has also played an important part in Simon's life with extensive travel around South East Asia, the USA, Central America and Mexico in recent years.

bronze
Simon Pemberton

03 Leith Harbour

Medium Mixed media

Brief Promote Edinburgh's Leigh Harbour development emphasising integration of old and new Commissioned by Nigel Hillier

Client Uffindell West

15

04

05

Russell Cobb

04   The Teacher

Medium   Acrylic

Brief   To illustrate a series of tarot cards depicting 10
different occupations, promoting The Guardian's
'Graduate Jobmatch'

Commissioned by   Giles Bernard

Client   The Guardian

Russell Cobb

05   The Designer

Medium   Acrylic

Brief   To illustrate a series of tarot cards depicting 10
different occupations, promoting The Guardian's
'Graduate Jobmatch'

Commissioned by   Giles Bernard

Client   The Guardian

Robyn Neild

06   Feisty Girl

Medium   Gouache, pen & ink

Brief   Independent, sexy, intense women

Commissioned by   Alice Koh

Client   Victoria's Secret

Images 29 **Advertising**

McFaul

07   Last Summer

Medium   Digital

Brief   Postcard promoting CIA's exhibition 'We Know
What You Did Last Summer' in NY Autumn 2004

Commissioned by   Louisa St Pierre

Client   Central Illustration Agency

Bob Venables

08   Chris Moyles Saviour

Medium   Alkyd

Brief   To portray Chris Moyles as heroic saviour
figure of breakfast radio

Commissioned by   Andy Jex

Agency   Fallon Advertising

Client   BBC

Andrew Bylo

09   Mile End Park

Medium   Gouache

Brief   Bright and lively image incorporating the new bridge
over Mile End Park

Commissioned by   Mike Walton

Client   London Transport Museum

10

11

Images 29 **Advertising**

Barry Downard

10 Café Distraction

Medium Digital

Brief To illustrate situations of 'Distraction' when the new
Mini convertible is around

Commissioned by Jane Scott

Agency Ptarmigan Consultants

Client BMW - Mini UK

Ian Pollock

11 Full Scream Ahead

Medium Mixed media

Brief Illustration for the London Dungeon, poster for
London Underground

Commissioned by Rob Hammond

Agency The Real Adventure

Client The London Dungeon

Jonas Bergstrand

12 CIA London Book Fair

Medium Digital

Brief Poster promoting illustration agency CIA
during the London Book Fair

Commissioned by Louisa St Pierre

Client Central Illustration Agency

13

Images 29 **Advertising**

Adam Graff

13 Walthamstow

Medium Digital

Brief To present Walthamstow as a desirable
destination highlighting the positive
aspects of the town

Commissioned by Rubie Charalambous

Client Waltham Forest Council

14

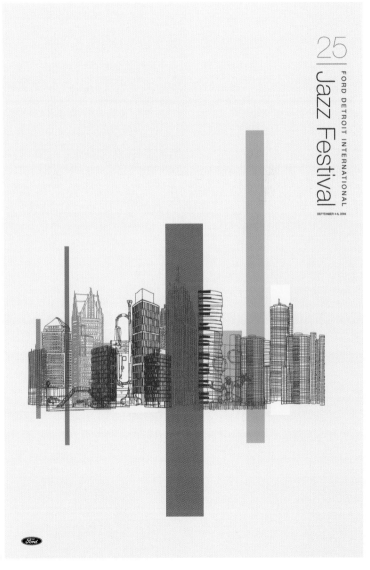

15

Xose Geada

14 Saturday Night

Medium Ed

Brief The background suggests the nightclub's name:
Keops. The main theme is the couple. He's courting
her but she's more interested in the club

Commissioned by Fatima Pan Medin

Agency Opción Gráfica

Client KEOPS Nightclub

Nick Reddyhoff

15 Ford Detroit International Jazz Festival

Medium Digital

Brief Detroit skyline for poster to advertise the festival

Commissioned by Matt Dimmer

Agency JWT Detroit

Client Ford Jazz Festival

16

Images 29 **Advertising**

Liz Myhill

16 Scottish Haddock

Medium Mixed media

Brief Poster to promote Scottish haddock within fish
and chip shops that should appeal to both retailers
and consumers

Commissioned by Josef Church

Client Seafood Scotland

Dylan Channon
Richard Krzyzak
Chris Wormell

design &
new media

Beach
Jim Chambers
Chris Corr
Charles Hively
Phill McVicar
Graham Rolfe

Gold

Lara Harwood

01 "L" for Litigation

Medium   Mixed media

Brief   Illustrate the word 'litigation' using the letter L

Commissioned by   Lippa Pearce

Client   Merchant Group LLP / Brunswick PR

After completing undergraduate studies in Graphics at Camberwell College of Art in 1989, Lara quickly established a broad client base. Her enthusiasm, love of colour and deft brushwork, coupled with assured application of ideas, has kept her in constant demand. She has numerous clients including The Sunday Times, The Saturday Times Magazine, the Sunday Telegraph, The New Yorker, New Scientist, VW Cars, IBM, Osborne Clarke Solicitors, Trigon, France Telecom, UNESCO, Elle (Germany), Ikea, Wolff Olins, Imperial Cancer Research and Amnesty International...

In parallel to her illustration career, Lara is a frequent exhibitor of works on canvas, monoprints and limited edition screenprints. "Being in touch with my personal work inspires fresh ways of thinking about illustration and that's a good thing."

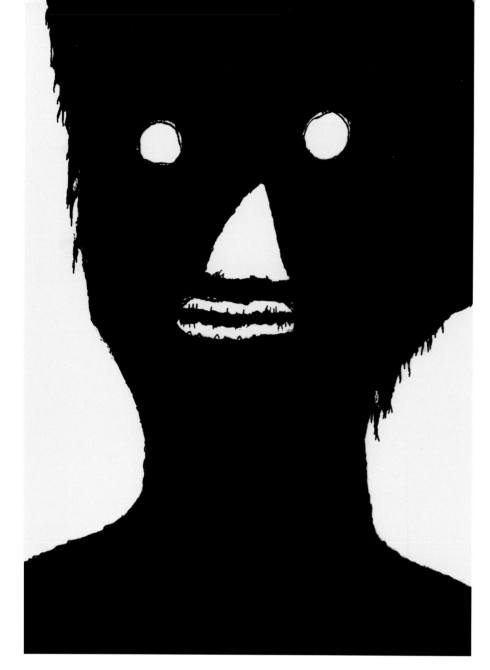

silver
Daryl Waller

02 Tom Violence

Medium Mixed media

Brief Design an interesting illustration to be reproduced onto a T-shirt

Client Uniqlo

Cornwall born Daryl Waller daydreamed and doodled his way through school and after studying illustration in Hereford he ended up at London's RCA where he completed his MA in Communication Art & Design in 2003.

In his early years some of his teachers were encouraging, but Daryl's unusual style caused a stir from the beginning. "I remember one teacher giving me hell because she'd asked everyone to paint a fire (bonfire night) and I just painted a massive piece of paper red, nothing else."

As well as his self-published books, Daryl collaborates with Cornish theatre company Kneehigh and film and theatre group o-region producing projections, programmes and artwork for their shows.

Daryl has been experimenting with moving image since his final year at the RCA and has shown many of his animations at o-region's monthly film night – 'Roughcut.'

Daryl has been working for magazines such as The World of Interiors, Marmalade, Stranger and Plan B Magazine...

Daryl had his first solo exhibition at London's A & D Gallery in Baker Street in August.

bronze
Ian Whadcock

03 Serco in Brief

Medium Digital

Brief To create a simple iconic strip of images to represent the 8 core business activities of Serco Group Worldwide

Commissioned by Duncan Moore

Client Pocknell Studios

Ian Whadcock has worked for 17 years as an illustrator - the commissions range across editorial, design and advertising clients in the UK and abroad. In the last 9 years he has worked increasingly via digital media - although the essential reason for being commissioned remains what happens on paper before he gets to the screen (i.e. the ability to think through a problem and put ideas down with a pencil). He aims to be commissioned for the way he approaches a problem and not necessarily just for a particular style of drawing.

Ian has also regularly lectured in Illustration most recently at Manchester Metropolitan University and Cambridge School of Art/APU and maintains an interest in the direction of Illustration education at undergraduate / post graduate levels.

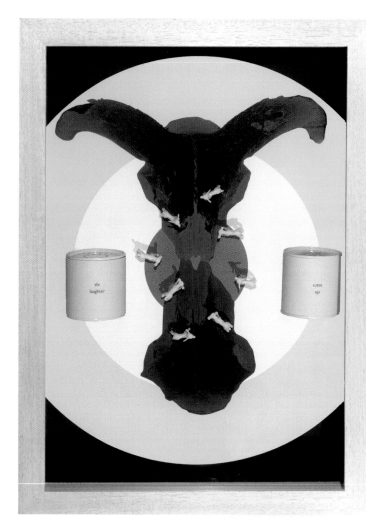

05

04

Andy Potts

04 Heathen Highway

Medium Digital

Brief To animate an illustration and provide a 22 step
tutorial for Computer Arts readers

Commissioned by Gillian Carson

Client Computer Arts

Gill Bradley

05 Bleating Heart

Medium Mixed media featuring canned 'bleats' triggered by
turning the award 180°

Brief Design an award for best use of sound effects in
animation for the British Animation Awards (BAA) to
combine Britain, sheep and animation

Commissioned by Jayne Pilling

Client British Animation Awards

Joanna Nelson

06 Ideas Incubator

Medium Mixed media

Brief Series of illustrations inspired by a poem written by Roger McGough

Commissioned by Jo Morrison

Client Nesta Futurelab

Joanna Nelson

07 Ideas Incubator

Medium Mixed media

Brief Series of illustrations inspired by a poem written by Roger McGough

Commissioned by Jo Morrison

Client Nesta Futurelab

08

Images 29 Design & New Media

Simon Stephenson

08 Van Gogh

Medium Digital

Brief Promote awareness of epilepsy through images
inspired by 'Van Gogh' for an exhibition called
'Homage to Van Gogh'

Client National Society for Epilepsy

09

Andrew Selby

09 Environment

Medium Digital

Brief Illustration promoting new shopping centres' desire to integrate into existing environments

commissioned by Andrew Hunter

Client Redpath

Pages per minute

Consumables

Paper Handling

Paper Weight

Print Driver

Oki Computers Printer Brochure

Jonathan Edwards

10   'Breathe Don't Stop' Mr On Vs The Jungle Bros

Medium   Pen & ink / digital

Brief   Street scene featuring Mr On and the Jungle Brothers
for a record and CD sleeve

Commissioned by   Hannah Neaves / Peter Chadwick

Client   EMI Music / Zip Design

Ian Whadcock

11   Jargon Buster

Medium   Digital

Brief   To bring humour and visual interest to the dull world
of technical jargon that surrounds buying a printer

Commissioned by   Mike Lackersteen

Client   Mike Lackersteen Design

13

Simon Pemberton

12 Talent Tree

Medium Mixed media

Brief Wrap around annual report cover to emphasise the
wealth of talent available within the company

Sarah McMenemy

13 Marylebone

Medium Mixed media

Brief To produce an illlustration of Marylebone High Street
for a brochure for Carter Jonas

Commissioned by Nick Paul

Client Archant Dialogue

14

Images 29 **Design & New Media**

Jonathan Cusick

14 Introducing the Orcadians

Medium Acrylic

Brief A mailshot booklet which built upon the storytelling
traditions of Orkney. Each portrait illustrated a short
story linking the islander with Highland Park Whisky

Commissioned by Lee Jackson

Client Navigator Responsive Advertising

15

16

Michelle Thompson

15 Headway - Running Boy

Medium Collage

Brief To produce an image inspired from the music to be used on the 12" single

Commissioned by Martin Yates

Client V2/Satellite

Neil Dimelow

16 Roof Garden, Manchester

Medium Digital

Brief To promote The Art Department's recently completed development in the Northern Quarter of Manchester - galleries and workspaces for artists and art organisations

Commissioned by Michael Trainor

Client The Art Department

17

Images 29 **Design & New Media**

Per José Karlén

17 M = maths

Medium Digital

Brief Illustrations for teaching (children) maths, with sound
and animation

Commissioned by Jens Peter de Pedro

Client Sveriges Utbildningsradio AB (UR)

18

Paul Wearing

18 Cocktails at Quaglinos

Medium Digital

Brief Capture the spirit of Quaglinos in a restaurant/bar
scene for a two metre high mural wrapping around a
column at the restaurant's main entrance

Commissioned by Conran Limited

Client Quaglinos

19

20

Lasse Skarbovik

19 King of Hearts

Medium Digital

Brief King of Hearts in a stock of cards

Commissioned by Lorraine Owen

Client The Organisation

Alan McGowan

20 Castle Fraser

Medium Pen and ink, watercolour

Brief To relate a National Trust for Scotland property to a person involved in working with that property; a dual portrait of both

Commissioned by Matt Chapman

Client Contagious Design

Alan McGowan

21 Ben Lomond

Medium Pen and ink, watercolour

Brief To relate a National Trust for Scotland property to a person involved in working with that property; a dual portrait of both

Commissioned by Matt Chapman

Client Contagious Design

41

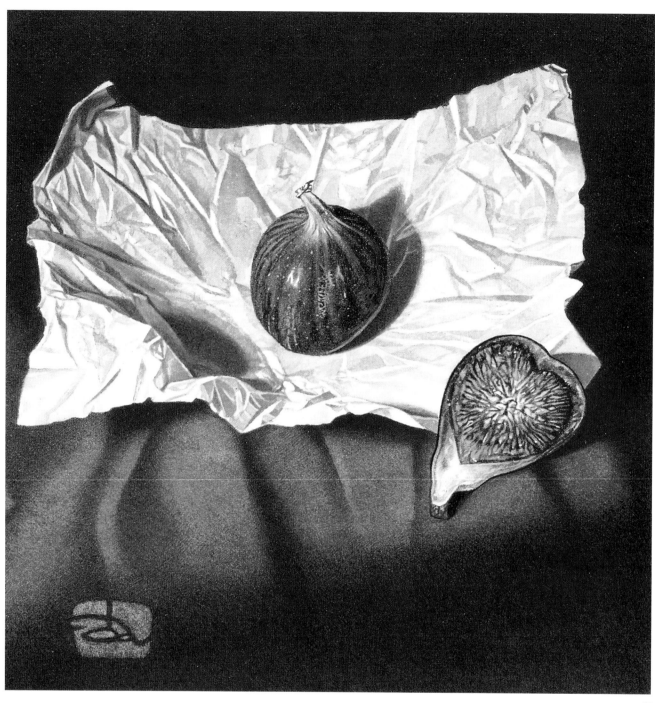

22

Images 29 **Design & New Media**

Darrell Warner

22 Fig

Medium Watercolour

Brief To produce a series of realistic and naturalistic
illustrations, featuring a subtle heart shape within the
subject matter

Commissioned by Lizzie Spivey

Client Heart of the Garden Publishing

Darrell Warner

23 Tristian

Medium Pencil

Brief To produce a final costume illustration following series
of concept drawings for the costume department for
the feature film, Arthur

Commissioned by Penny Rose

Client Disney Pictures

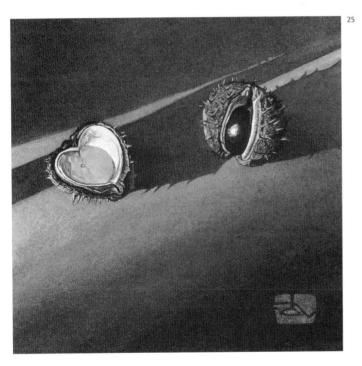

Darrell Warner

24   Arthur

Medium   Pencil, ink & bleach wash

Brief   To produce a final battle dress illustration following series of concept drawings for the costume department for the feature film, Arthur

Commissioned by   Penny Rose

Client   Disney Pictures

Darrell Warner

25   Conker

Medium   Watercolour

Brief   To produce a series of realistic and naturalistic illustrations, featuring a subtle heart shape within the subject matter

Commissioned by   Lizzie Spivey

Client   Heart of the Garden Publishing

Darrell Warner

26   Bors

Medium   Pencil, ink & bleach wash

Brief   To produce a final battle dress illustration following series of concept drawings for the costume department for the feature film, Arthur

Commissioned by   Penny Rose

Client   Disney Pictures

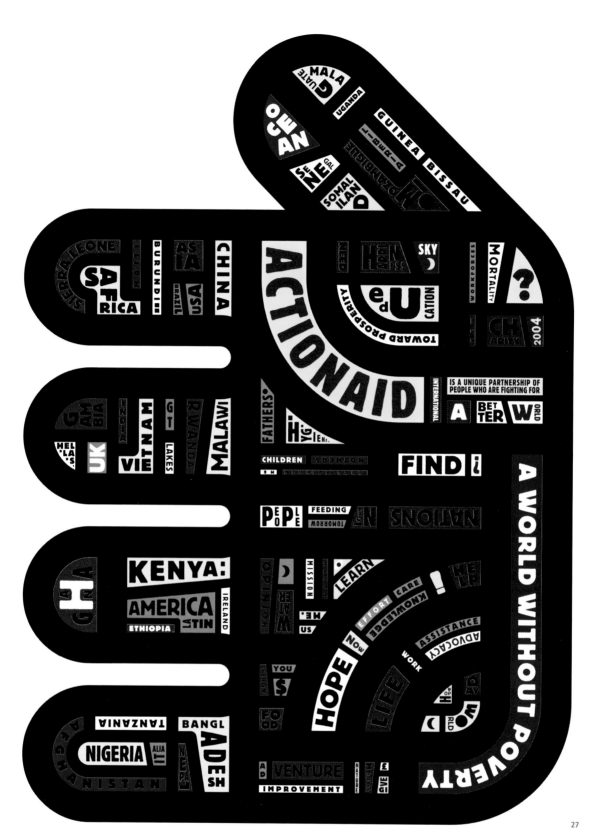

Images 29 **Design & New Media**

Peter Grundy

27 Hand

Medium Digital

Brief Design a poster to promote Action Aid

Commissioned by Dilhan Attanyake

Client Action Aid International

Mulling Spice
Room Spray

Citrus
Handwash

Cucumber
Handwash

Craig Bennett

28   Mintie/9-Lives+

Medium   Mixed media

Brief   Album sleeve for Bristol band Mintie using graffiti / hip-hop culture as a starting point and Mintie colours

Commissioned by   Cerise Reed

Client   Aardvark Creative

Sarah Gibb

29   Cooks Range Characters

Medium   Watercolour

Brief   To produce 6 characters for a new range of products for cooks

Commissioned by   Robin Anderson

Client   Crabtree & Evelyn

Images 29 **Design & New Media**

Russell Cobb

30 Call for Entries

Medium Acrylic

Brief To produce a cover image for Images 29 Call for
Entries form. To depict the key stages of the creative
process, observation, ideas and creation

Client AOI

Peter Horridge

31 Accounts

Medium Pen, ink & digital

Brief An image combining illustration and calligraphy for
the section title pages of an annual report for Gard, a
shipping insurance company

Commissioned by Bjørn Høydal

Client Trigger AS, Norway

Images 29 **Design & New Media**

Kate Newington

32 Nicola

Medium Paper fragments, pen & digital media

Brief To make a portrait of Yvonne Davis's daughter, Nicola,
using scraps and fragments of printed, plain or
textured paper

Commissioned by Yvonne Davis

Royal Mail Mint Stamps

Satoshi Kambayashi

33 Occasions

Medium Mixed media

Brief To produce a set of stamps that encourage 'social mail'

Commissioned by Catharine Brandy, Marcus James

Client Royal Mail Group plc

Craig Thomson

34 Halloweenies

Medium Digital

Brief Create characters for a range of Halloween
confectionery and point of sale displays

Commissioned by Julie Scrutton

Client Kinnerton Confectionery

editorial

Crispian Brown
Roger Browning
Andrew Foster
Chris Kasch
Alison Lawn
Amanda Scope

Gold

Nick Dewar

01 Identity Theft

Medium Acrylic

Brief Illustrate an article about the growing crime of identity theft

Commissioned by Martin Colyer / Hugh Kyle

Client Reader's Digest

Nick Dewar was born in Scotland. He grew up in a small fishing town on the East Coast and attended art school in Glasgow. Since then he has lived in Prague, London and on a sheep farm in Cumbria. Currently, Nick lives in New York.

His work has appeared in magazines, on billboards, in books and next to the telephone.

Nick admires the work of Tom Friedman, Earl Oliver Hurst and Ivor Cutler. However inspiration mostly comes from crackly music and wandering about in a perpetual daze.

His spare time is spent putting lint into strangers' pockets.

He likes to think of himself as surviving a brutal 'Kes'-style Northern schooling. But as his photo clearly shows, he was able to rise above the beatings and ritual humiliations through the magic that is illustration.

52

silver

Kevin Hauff

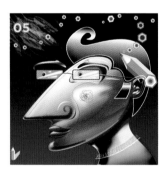

02 Pension Strength

Medium Digital / mixed

Brief Illustration for the Money Observer Magazine on a theme of pension management, including guidance for choosing a fund with maximum strength for future return

Commissioned by Ellie Rudolf

Client Money Observer Magazine

After studying illustration at Brighton, Kevin Hauff entered into the commercial world. An early break came with receiving the "Best Newcomer" Award from the AOI, which considerably raised his profile. Having previously had agency representation, Kevin is currently 'self represented' with a new collective called 741 Illustration. To date he has worked with numerous interesting and assorted clients including Royal Mail Stamps, Radio Times, New Scientist, Barclays Bank and The Economist.

A sketchbook, paint and collage have been the primary mediums for making images, playing with many different approaches, but a recent weapon of choice has been the computer. A new digital style has evolved incorporating the use of paint and collage, paving the way for a fresh new direction. Paint will never be abandoned as a medium, but it can now be combined with the versatility and freedom of the computer.

four eyes

Paul Blow

03 Too Shy
Medium Mixed media
Brief Illustrate an article about overcoming shyness
Commissioned by Martin Colyer
Client Reader's Digest

bronze

Paul Blow was born in Falkirk, Scotland but grew up in Lyme Regis, Dorset. As a thinly disguised Englishman he soon realised his need to draw.

He studied illustration at Maidstone College of Art and then Brighton and still in disguise passed himself off as an illustrator.

He has been nominated for a Glenfiddich Food and Drink Award and received Silver in the Transport for London Poster competition – Simply Culture ,and now a Bronze Award in Images 29.

His clients in the UK and US include Royal Mail, The Guardian, The FT, Independent, Time Magazine, Reader's Digest, BBC Worldwide, Management Today, Carter Wong & Tomlin, The New Scientist, Popular Science, Fortune & Small Business Magazine, Harvard Business Review, Advertising Age, LA Magazine, Philadelphia Magazine and Saatchi & Saatchi.

He divides his time between his family, drawing and keeping up the English pretence.

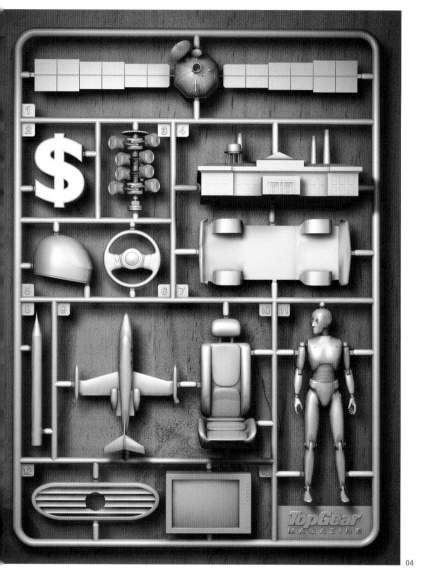

05

Images 29 **Editorial**

Engine - Matthew Key

04 Top Gear Magazine Model Kit

Medium Digital

Brief Illustrate 13 items in a model kit. Each item relates to
that months subject with each item being popped out
when used

Commissioned by Charlie Turner

Client BBC Worldwide

Andy Potts

05 Design Week Top 100

Medium Digital

Brief To design a cover that conveyed the message of the
Top 100 Design Businesses in competition using the
visual metaphor of construction and architecture

Commissioned by Ivan Cottrell

Client Design Week

06

Nigel Buchanan

06 Partridge

Medium Digital

Brief To illustrate the 12 days of Christmas

Commissioned by Alex Nicholas

Client Radio Times

Matt Lee

07 High Brow, Low Rent

Medium Mixed media

Brief The Opera costs a tenner, but a football ticket is £50.
The cult of celebrity is turning London into a cultural
bargain basement

Commissioned by Andrew Lee

Client FT Magazine

08

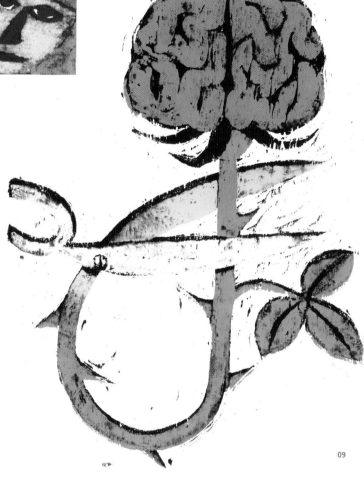
09

Daniel Pudles

08 Breaking Waves

Medium Mixed media

Brief Review of 'Star of the Sea ' by Joseph O'Connor, a
crime novel set on a ship in mid-19th century Britain

Commissioned by Una Corrigan

Client The Economist

Daniel Pudles

09 Mind and Matter

Medium Mixed media

Brief A.S. Byatt on the feeling brain and the thinking body.
Illustration for The Review cover

Commissioned by Roger Browning

Client The Guardian

Daniel Pudles

10 Break Out the Bicycles

Medium Mixed media

Brief To illustrate how the West is deluding itself over oil
resources, for the Comment and Analysis page

Commissioned by Roger Browning

Client The Guardian

Images 29 **Editorial**

Nishant Choksi

11   Growing Pains

Medium   Digital

Brief   In the aftermath of the dotcom boom, companies are
re-assessing the role of the technology incubator

Commissioned by   Paul Martin

Client   IEE Review

Nishant Choksi

12   European Microelectronics

Medium   Digital

Brief   Money! is what the European microelectronics firms
want from their government

Commissioned by   Paul Martin

Client   IEE Review

Andy Ward

13   Euro 2004 Fantasy XI

Medium   Digital

Brief   To illustrate the players featured in Radio Times Euro 2004 Fantasy XI

Commissioned by   Jamie Trendall

Client   Radio Times

Mel Croft

14   The Gourd Life

Medium   Mixed media

Brief   'With Love From' monthly feature. Article about Austrian pumpkin seed oil and the husband and wife teams who produce it

Commissioned by   Brian Saffer

Client   Waitrose Food Illustrated - John Brown Citrus Publishing

Mel Croft

15   Golfers

Medium   Mixed media

Brief   To illustrate an article about the various characters to be found on a golf driving range

Commissioned by   Hayden Russell

Client   Total Golf Magazine - IPC Media

16

17

Alastair Taylor

16 What the World Needs Now

Medium Acrylic

Brief Since 9/11 war on terrorism has dominated
the global agenda

Commissioned by Yvonne McCrimmon

Client Time Magazine

Jackie Parsons

17 Untitled

Medium Mixed media

Brief To convey the idea of losing oneself in a different
world whilst reading on the tube or in public places

Commissioned by Elissa Millhouse

Client The Independent on Saturday

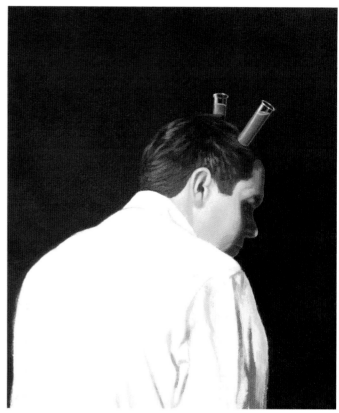

Images 29 **Editorial**

James Fryer

18 Slow Transfers

Medium Acrylic

Brief Bank transfers not only take too long but you lose
money in that time as well

Commissioned by Paul Hollington

Client The Sunday Times, Money section

James Fryer

19 Bailing Out

Medium Acrylic

Brief Equities are in a bad state and so people are bailing
out and joining Hedge Funds

Commissioned by Colin McHenry

Client Fund Strategy Magazine, Centaur Communications

James Fryer

20 The Science Scaremongers

Medium Acrylic

Brief Instead of helping and reassuring the public, scientists
have a knack of creating confusion and uncertainty in
an already paranoid world

Commissioned by Steve Place

Client The Times Educational Supplement

James Fryer

21 Status Anxiety

Medium Acrylic

Brief To illustrate the way in which people worry about their status in life

Commissioned by Jamie Trendall

Client Radio Times, BBC Worldwide Publications

James Fryer

22 Computer Virus Protection

Medium Acrylic

Brief Should internet service providers provide virus protection?

Commissioned by Bill Bagnall

Client Computer Buyer Magazine, Dennis Publishing

23

Images 29 **Editorial**

Louise Weir

23 Special Brew

Medium Acrylic

Brief Portrait of Robert Wyatt who creates strange worlds
within his music

Commissioned by Mark Wagstaff

Client Mojo

24

25

Linda Scott

24 Storyteller

Medium Acrylic

Brief Storytelling is being re-introduced and
encouraged as an important activity by both
teachers and parents. Particular emphasis is
to be placed on folk tales and mythology

Commissioned by Margaret Donegan

Client Times Educational Supplement

Matthew Johnson

25 Cooking up Conflict

Medium Mixed media

Brief Show conflict between kitchen designers and
architects over the professional issue of demarcation
of roles

Commissioned by Patrick Myles

Client ETP Publishing

26

A. Richard Allen

26   Ghosts

Medium   Ink & digital

Brief   Linking two features, one about supernatural problems
with homes, the other about more earthly issues such
as noisy neighbours

Commissioned by   Mike Krage

Client   The Times: Bricks and Mortar

A. Richard Allen

27 Anger Management

Medium Ink & digital

Brief The author tries to tackle his anger management
issues whilst in New York by enrolling for a course
of therapy

Commissioned by Andy Chappin

Client Financial Times

A. Richard Allen

28 Bull and Bear

Medium Ink & digital

Brief Feature looking at the current state of the stockmarket
and whether it's better at present to be a 'bull'
or a 'bear'

Commissioned by Ben Brannan

Client Esquire Magazine

29

30

Images 29 **Editorial**

Chris Robson

29   Euro Film Stereotypes

Medium   Digital

Brief   Map of Europe with national stereotypes used in
Hollywood films

Commissioned by   Richard Scott

Client   Future Publishing

Lasse Skarbovik

30   Flash

Medium   Digital

Brief   Illustration in Computer Arts about how to work
with Flash

Client   Computer Arts

Daryl Waller

31 Xiu Xiu

Medium Mixed media

Brief To illustrate the interview of the band 'Xiu Xiu' for the
new magazine Plan B

Commissioned by Andrew Clare

Client Plan B

Ian Pollock

32   Guts

Medium   Mixed media

Brief   Illustration for short story by Chuck Palahniuk

Commissioned by   Maggie Murphy

Client   The Guardian Weekend

Andrew Baker

33 Senses of the Blind

Medium Digital

Brief How blind people can use four senses to appreciate
the aesthetics of the world around them

Commissioned by Alex Nicholas

Client BBC Worldwide

Andrew Baker

34 Nanobots

Medium Digital

Brief To illustrate how nanotechnology has made
microscopic robots a reality. Is the technology in
safe hands?

Commissioned by Alex Nicholas

Client BBC Worldwide

35

Lucie Sheridan

35   Untitled

Medium   Mixed media

Brief   Tourists speaking the language when travelling abroad

Commissioned by   Gavin Brammall

Client   The Observer Travel Magazine

36

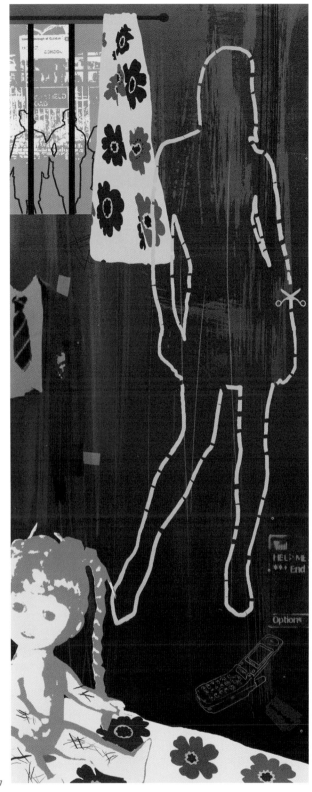

37

C F Payne

36 The Escape Artist

Medium Mixed media

Brief Blair shrugs off threats to his job,
puts the BBC back in their box

Commissioned by Paul Lussier

Client Time Magazine

Marina Caruso

37 Self Harm

Medium Digital

Brief Article about the rise of self harming among
teenage girls

Commissioned by Jane Berry

Client Associated Newspaper

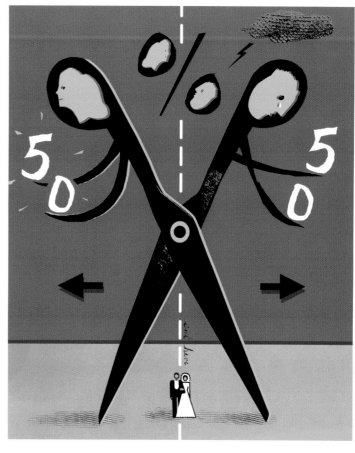

Frazer Hudson

38   Card Swipe

Medium   Digital

Brief   Represent identity theft

Commissioned by   Martin Harrison

Client   The Times

Frazer Hudson

39   50/50 Divorce Split

Medium   Digital

Brief   Create a full page illustration which graphically communicates the idea of equal cuts for men and women during divorce settlement

Commissioned by   Jessica Reiter

Client   The Mail on Sunday

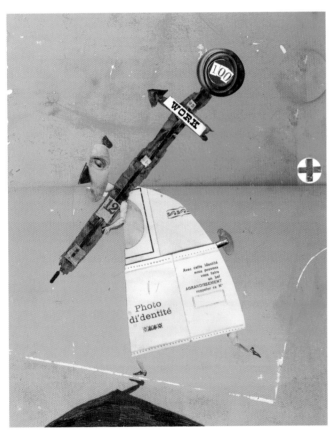

40

Ben Hawkes

40 Martyrdom at Work

Medium Collage

Brief Illustrate an article on employers' increasingly
unsympathetic attitude towards the common cold and
the culture of martyrdom it creates

Commissioned by Katie Ramsay

Client First4Business.Co.Uk Ltd

Carolyn Gowdy

41 Stabbed

Medium Mixed media

Brief The angel arrives in time to provide protection and to
call for an end to the violence. For a short story set in
South Africa

Commissioned by Lucy Vickery

Client The Spectator

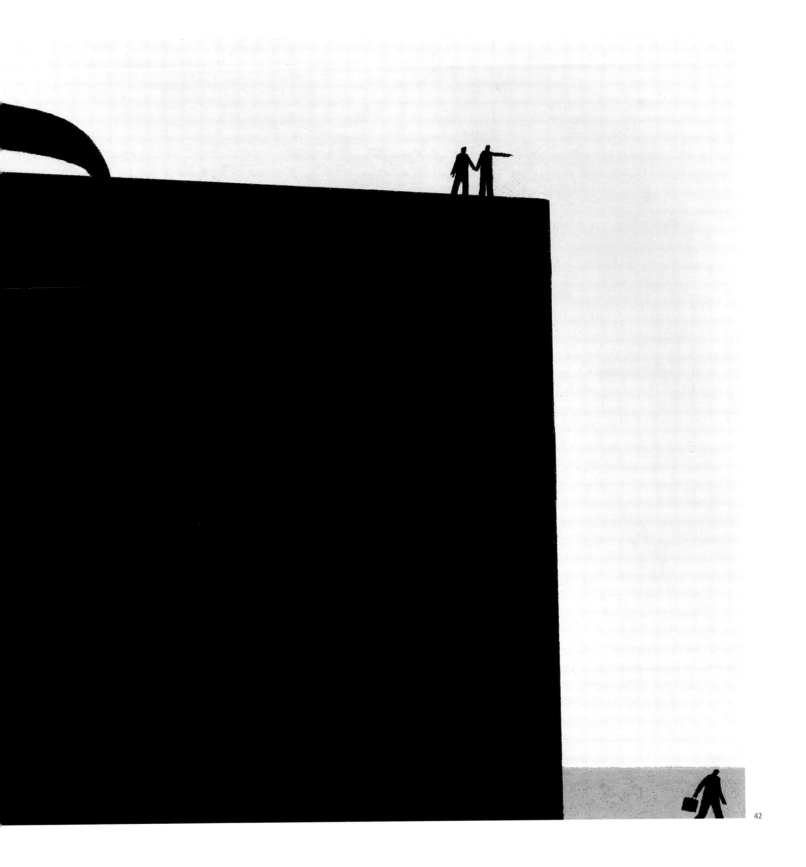

42

Images 29 **Editorial**

43

44

Geoff Grandfield

43 Where are the Police?

Medium Pastel

Brief Illustrate an article about the police being bogged
down by paperwork

Commissioned by Martin Colyer

Client Reader's Digest

Geoff Grandfield

44 Rising House

Medium Pastel

Brief Short story involving female narrator opposing
building development of childhood playground. Leads
to unexpected twist

Commissioned by Andy Chappin

Client Financial Times

Images 29 **Editorial**

Stuart Briers

45 Reputation

Medium Digital

Brief To evoke the spirit of excellence and imaginative
development of a pharmaceutical company

Commissioned by Nick Reed

Client Spirit Magazine

46

47

Stuart Briers

46 Creating the Union

Medium Digital

Brief To accompany an article about how the European
Union was formed

Commissioned by Sara Wadsworth

Client Financial Times

Stephen Collins

47 Care Home Funding

Medium Mixed media & Photoshop

Brief To illustrate a letter complaining about the lack of
funding for care homes for the elderly

Commissioned by Parminder Bahra

Client The Times

48

49

Images 29 **Editorial**

Michelle Thompson

48 Children in Care

Medium Digital

Brief Children in care

Commissioned by Lawrence Bogle

Client Times Educational Supplement / Friday Magazine

Garry Parsons

49 Giant Salaries

Medium Digital

Brief False promises for nurses

Commissioned by Richard Davies

Client RCN Publishing

50

51

Future Beckham Haircuts; The Bull, The Zinedine, The Spanish Inquisition

Matthew Cook

50 Building

Medium Watercolour

Brief As war artist for The Times to record the Gulf War 2003

Commissioned by David Driver

Client The Times

Jonas Bergstrand

51 Future Beckham Haircuts

Medium Digital

Brief Beckham caricatures

Commissioned by Will Harvey

Client Sorted Magazine

Frank Love

52 Parole

Medium Mixed media

Brief Depict a case study of a man who has failed
parole for 25 years

Commissioned by Andy Martin

Client Radio Times

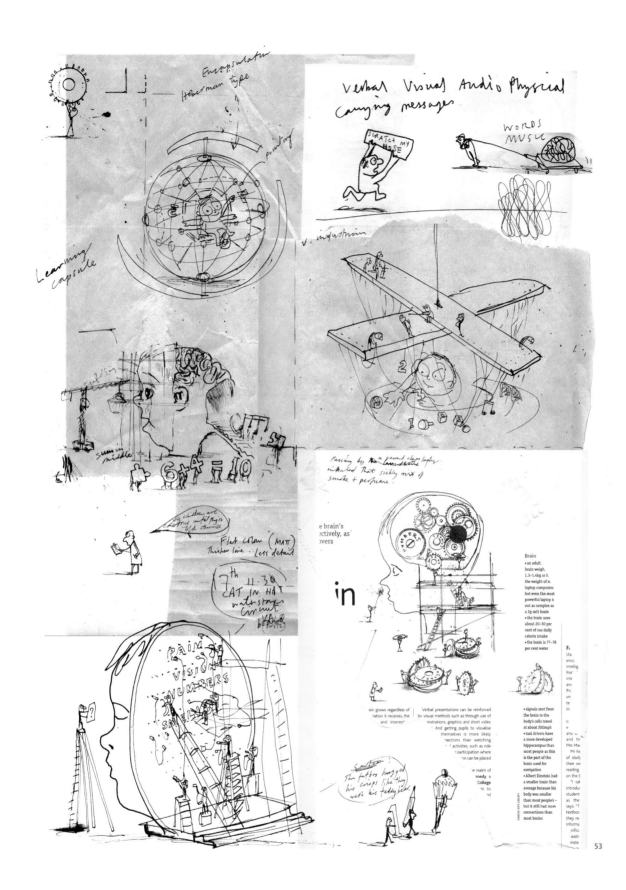

Simon Spilsbury

53 Brain Child

Medium Pen

Brief Illustrate how a child's brain develops and works

Commissioned by Rozzy Secret

Client Redwood

55

54

Images 29 **Editorial**

Adrian Johnson

54 Stress in the Workplace

Medium Mixed media

Brief To illustrate an article on the EAP

Commissioned by Deborah Ford

Client Estate Gazette

Paul Willoughby

55 Dennis Wilson

Medium Mixed media

Brief One in a series of eight pictures produced to illustrate
the 'lost weekends' of several celebrities

Commissioned by Declan Fahy

Client Jack Magazine

James Marsh

56 Christmas Cover

Medium Acrylic

Brief To illustrate the Radio Times Christmas and
New Year cover 2003-2004

Commissioned by Shem Law

Client Radio Times

57

Belle Mellor

57 Sand Grinder

Medium Mixed media

Brief For The Guardian 'Summer Cartoon Special'

Commissioned by Paul Howlett

Client The Guardian

Belle Mellor

58 Post Natal Depression

Medium Mixed media

Brief For an article by a woman who had suffered from post
natal depression

Commissioned by Roger Browning

Client The Guardian

Satoshi Kambayashi

59   Playing with Fire

Medium   Mixed media

Brief   America's Twin Mortgage giants have accounting problems

Commissioned by   Una Corrigan

Client   The Economist

Satoshi Kambayashi

60   Come Out and Play

Medium   Mixed media

Brief   Linux's challenge to Bill Gates' Windows OS

Commissioned by   Una Corrigan

Client   The Economist

Satoshi Kambayashi

61   Cruel Entertainment

Medium   Pen and ink (line and wash)

Brief   Our adult oriented culture exploits the real needs of children

Commissioned by   Mike Topp

Client   The Guardian

Satoshi Kambayashi

62 Playing with Fire 2

Medium Mixed media

Brief Leveraged funds of Hedge Funds may be less independent of each other, making the risk a sector-wide one

Commissioned by Penny Garrett

Client The Economist

Jonathan Cusick

63 The Sermon on the Mount

Medium Acrylic

Brief A priest is asked to hold £3,000 by a gambling parishioner during confession. Temptation gets the better of the priest with dire consequences

Commissioned by Alex Nicholas

Client BBC Worldwide Ltd

64

Jonathan Burton

64   Conspiracy Conference

Medium   Pen and ink (line and wash)

Brief   Illustrate the kind of people that might attend a
conspiracy theorist's conference

Commissioned by   Etienne Gilfillan

Client   Fortean Times

65

66

67

Jonathan Burton

65 Slick

Medium Mixed media

Brief Illustrate the problem of a woman who is regularly left alone unable to make a connection with her husband

Commissioned by Richard Eccleston & Caroline McGivern

Client The Observer

Roberto Parada

66 Beach Blanket Brawl

Medium Oils

Brief Kicking sand at the Germans, Berlusconi and ministers prove ugly old stereotypes are alive

Commissioned by Paul Lussier

Client Time Magazine

Andrew Davidson

67 QM II

Medium Gouache

Brief To accompany an article about the maiden voyage of QM II

Commissioned by Martin Harrison

Client The Times

68

Simon Pemberton

68   Little Devil

Medium   Mixed media

Brief   Produced for The Observer Living article about
demonising other people's children

Client   The Observer

Rod Hunt

69 Building Ethical Corporations

Medium   Digital

Brief   Design a cover image to get across the idea of ethical
corporations being built in the City

ommissioned by   Mariel Faulds

Client   Cross Border Publishing

Jane Webster

70 Eat Out Cover

Medium   Mixed media

Brief   Cover for 'Eat Out for £5' promotional supplement -
The Times

Commissioned by   Martin Harrison

Client   The Times Newspaper

71

72

Adam Graff

71   Techno-Protesters

Medium   Digital

Brief   To depict the current trend of protesters who are now
using the internet to gain support for their cause

Commissioned by   John Farley

Client   Daily Telegraph

Adam Graff

72   Self HELP!

Medium   Digital

Brief   To present the negative aspect of a saturated self help
market

Commissioned by   Sue Thomas

Client   Sunday Star Times

McFaul

73 Hair

Medium Digital

Brief To illustrate why hair on someone's head is all right
but when it turn's up in someone's soup it's
disgusting

Commissioned by Alex Nicholas

Client Radio Times

McFaul

74 Investor in People

Medium Digital

Brief To illustrate an article on the subject of people's
investment in business (mono)

Commissioned by Tony Mullins

Client Financial Times

Images 29 **Editorial**

Ian Whadcock

75 Indispensables

Medium Digital

Brief To illustrate how people still do not trust the lift, seeing them as spooky and given to fatal free-fall plummeting

Commissioned by Alex Nicholas

Client Radio Times

Ian Whadcock

76 The Search for Female Viagra

Medium Digital

Brief Article on the race to find a female equivalent to the male Viagra pill

Commissioned by Sue Vago

Client Economist Group

Ian Whadcock

77 The Bretton Woods Widows at 60

Medium Digital

Brief To show how the 'sisters' (the IMF and the World Bank) are treated like a 'pinata' at their own party to celebrate 60 years since their formation in 1944

Commissioned by Una Corrigan

Client Economist Group

Images 29 **Editorial**

Mark Thomas

78 Dr Who Cover

Medium Acrylic

Brief To illustrate the 40th anniversary of Dr Who

Commissioned by Paul Smith

Client Radio Times

RadioTimes

OLYMPICS 2004

**YOUR DAY-BY-DAY TV GUIDE TO THE GAMES,
INCLUDING FULL INTERACTIVE LISTINGS!
PLUS: THE PUNDITS' PICK OF THE ONES TO WATCH**

Mark Thomas

79 Olympics 2004

Medium Acrylic

Brief To illustrate the cover of Radio Times
Olympics supplement

Commissioned by Paul Smith

Client Radio Times

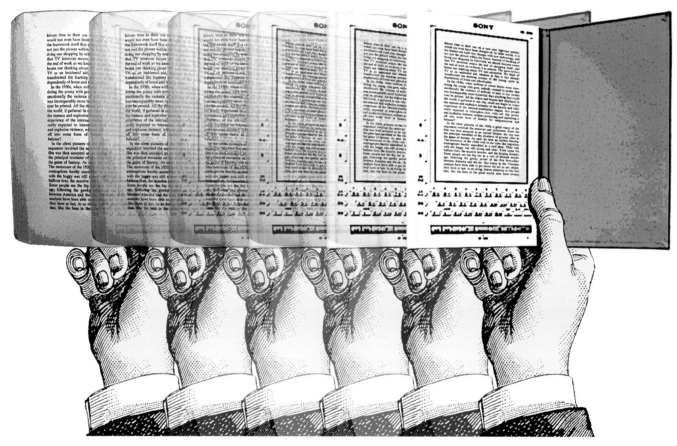

80

Images 29 **Editorial**

Jovan Djordjevic

80 Read All About It!

Medium Mixed media

Brief Transition from the printed word to the digital word
via e-books

Commissioned by Steve Place

Client Times Educational Supplement

81

82

Paul Bommer

81 Fat American Fridges

Medium Digital

Brief To illustrate an article about the increasing popularity of the huge American style fridge in the UK and the corresponding increase in waistlines

Commissioned by Roger Browning

Client The Guardian

Paul Bommer

82 Hospital Radio

Medium Digital

Brief To illustrate an article about a South London hospital outreach program of recruitment from local ethnic communities

Commissioned by Dennis Sterne

Client Health Service Journal

84

Images 29 **Editorial**

Paul Blow

83 Virgin Gardener

Medium Mixed media

Brief How a first time gardener tackles her first ever garden

Commissioned by Jane Bramwell

Client Seven Publishing

Philip Wrigglesworth

84 Mind Changers

Medium Acrylic

Brief A radio programme discussing the psychology of agreeing with a group, even if you know they're wrong

Commissioned by Alex Nicholas

Client BBC Worldwide

83

85

86

Philip Wrigglesworth

85 Give Us the Railways We Deserve

Medium Acrylic

Brief Article suggesting drastic action is needed to reform
who controls the railways

ommissioned by Hugh Kyle

Client RD Publications

Philip Wrigglesworth

86 The Pleasure Seekers

Medium Acrylic

Brief Feature discussing the brain's hedonistic tendencies in
the search for happiness

Commissioned by Craig Mackie

Client New Scientist

87

Images 29 **Editorial**

Jonathan Williams

87 How the Chips were Won

Medium Mixed media

Brief Portrait of Craig Barrett (CEO of Intel) whose dry wit, calculated reticence and interest in horseriding invites comparison with Clint Eastwood

Commissioned by Matthew Runeare

Client Time Warner

Jonathan Williams

88 Eisner's Exit Strategy

Medium Mixed media

Brief As Disney's embattled CEO prepares for the end game
of his long and controversial reign, Business 2.0 offers
an exit strategy

Commissioned by Mimi Dutta

Client Time Warner

Images 29 **Editorial**

Henning Löhlein

89 Fast Food Industry in the Dock

Medium Acrylic

Brief Cover illustration about obesity litigation in the US

Commissioned by R Smith

Client Lexis Nexis

Henning Löhlein

90 Mixed Faith Parents

Medium Acrylic

Brief Illustrating the problems children can have who grow
up in mixed faith families

Commissioned by R Smith

Client Lexis Nexis

Images 29 **Editorial**

Brett Ryder

91 Clever Trees

Medium Digital

Brief To illustrate trees being smarter than you think.
Some can water themselves and others can even wave
their branches

Commissioned by Alex Nicholas

Client Radio Times

Tim Ellis

92 Sound Pollution

Medium Digital

Brief To illustrate how scientists are trying to find ways to
help us live with a world that is noisier than ever

Commissioned by Alex Nicholas

Client Radio Times

93

John Bradley

93 Evil Mobile

Medium Digital

Brief Illustrate an article on the demonisation of mobile
phones with various health scares

Commissioned by Susha Lee-Shothaman

Client Prospect Magazine

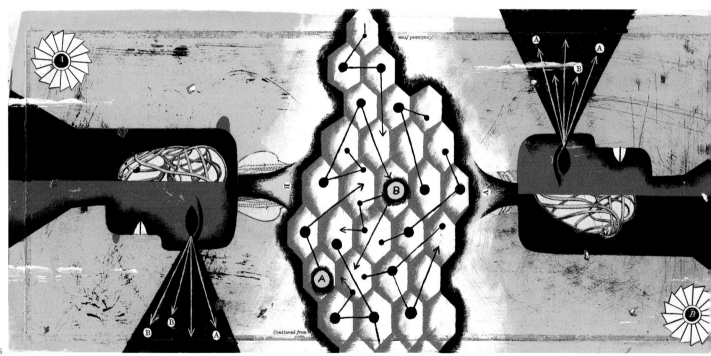

Images 29 **Editorial**

Russell Cobb

94 Behind the Mask

Medium Acrylic

Brief One of a series of illustrations produced for a mind
reading special feature. How research is uncovering
our motivations, desires and prejudices

Commissioned by Alison Lawn

Client New Scientist

Russell Cobb

95 Private Thoughts Public Property

Medium Acrylic

Brief One of a series of illustrations produced for a mind
reading special feature. Revealing personal desires
and prejudices

Commissioned by Alison Lawn

Client New Scientist

Russell Cobb

96 Why We Do What We Do

Medium Acrylic

Brief One of a series produced for a mind reading
special feature. About predicting the choices people
are making

Commissioned by Alison Lawn

Client New Scientist

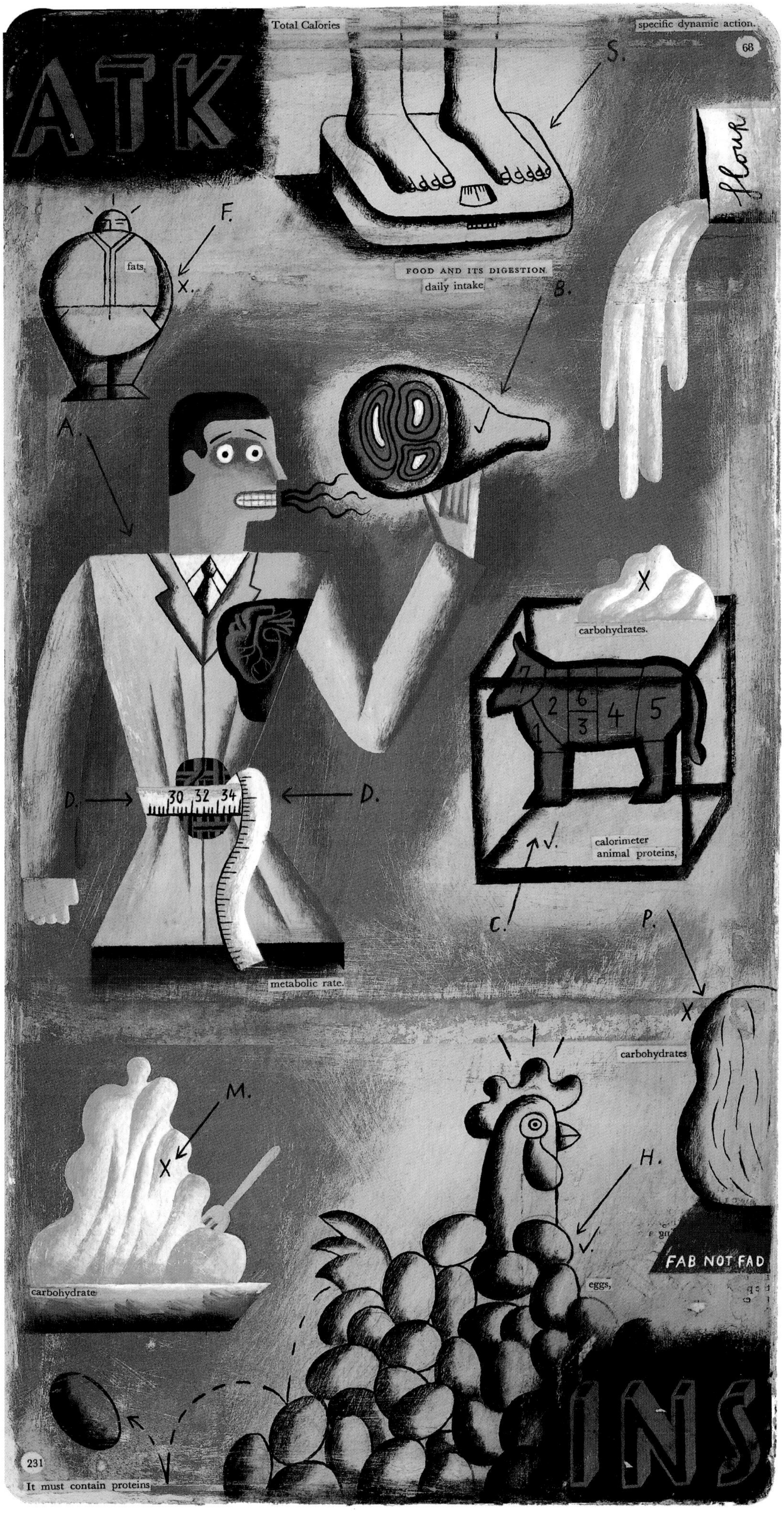

Russell Cobb

97 The Atkins Revolution

Medium Acrylic

Brief To illustrate an article about the winners and the losers of the Atkins diet

Commissioned by Johnathan Christie

Client The Independent on Sunday

98

99

Engine - Dan Smith

98   Golive vs Dreamweaver

Medium   Mixed media

Brief   2 pieces of software (Golive and Dreamweaver)
battling it out for the best internet software title

Commissioned by   Aston Leach

Client   Dennis Publishing

Jon Berkeley

99   John Goodman

Medium   Acrylic

Brief   Life mirrors art: Speaker John Goodman is sworn in as
VP in The West Wing, while in Washington succession
rules are under discussion

Commissioned by   Allan Comport / Bonnie Benwick

Client   The Washington Post

100

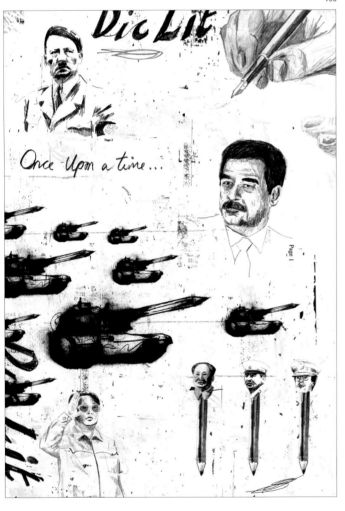

101

Scott Chambers

100 They Lived Happily Ever After

Medium Pencil

Brief To illustrate the phrase 'Dit-Lit', Dictator-Literature, people with absolute power writing for their captive audience, who want power and praise

Commissioned by Andrew Lee

Client Financial Times

Ric Machin

101 Rowan Atkinson

Medium Mixed media

Brief Commissioned by The Times for article in their Arts section

Commissioned by Sue Foll

Client The Times

102

103

Images 29 **Editorial**

Paul Slater

102 Sounds of Nature

Medium Acrylic

Brief To illustrate the weird and wonderful sounds of the
natural world

Commissioned by Alex Nicholas

Client Radio Times

Neil Shrubb

103 The Men of Manchester

Medium Digital

Brief Turn seven crappy reference photos into a moody
group of Manchester's movers and shakers

Commissioned by Richard Krzyzak

Client Property Week

104

105

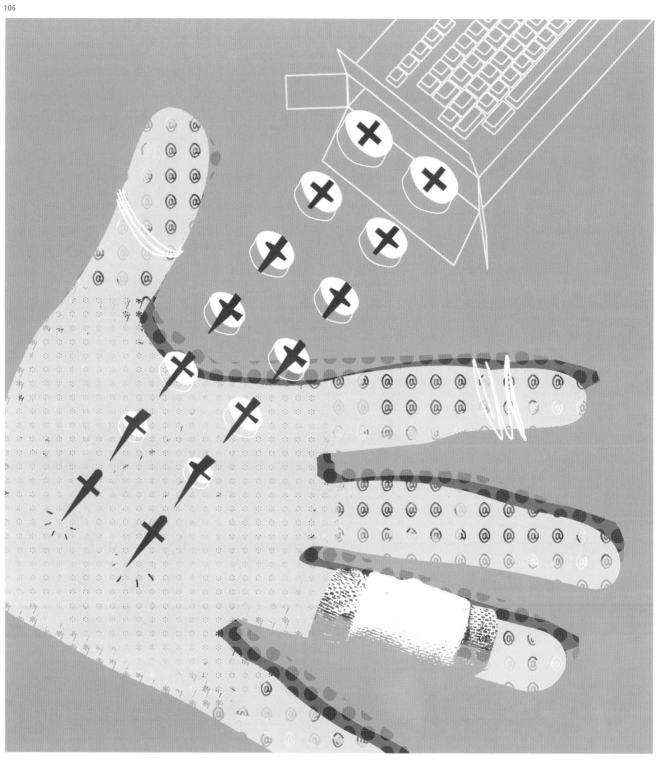

Images 29 **Editorial**

Nicholas Carn

106 Online Pharmacies

Medium Digital

Brief Illustrate an article on the dangers of buying medicine
on the internet

Commissioned by Martin Colyer / Hugh Kyle

Client Reader's Digest

Beach

107 Property Piracy

Medium Mixed media

Brief Illustrate a piece on the difficulties of buying and
selling houseboats

Commissioned by Jon Farley

Client Daily Telegraph Newspaper

Images 29 **Editorial**

Chris Watson

108 Marilyn Manson

Medium Mixed media

Brief Full page illustration of rock singer Marilyn Manson for
Bang Magazine

Commissioned by Danny Gloom

Client Future Publishing

children's books

Anna Billson

Martin Colyer

Lisa Kopper

Sarah McMenemy

Sarah Mears

Fred van Deelen was born in Holland and attended the Rotterdamse Grafische School where he trained as an artworker/designer with illustration as a main interest. In 1988 he moved to Austria where he found work in Linz in a small studio as an illustrator. There, he became proficient in a broad range of techniques (pen and ink/pencil/airbrush/painting...) and helped popularise traditional scraperboard/woodcut techniques in the Austrian advertising and design world.

Following this, he arrived in the UK in 1993 with an extensive portfolio and was happily taken on by The Organisation agency. Since then, he has worked with many of the big advertising agencies, design companies and publishing houses and says that having a varied portfolio has been a saviour in such a competitive market.

In 1998, Fred finally acquired his first computer which enabled him to diversify further and introduce more styles to his repertoire. He is now based in France, and thanks to email, is able to work much as before.

Fred van Deelen

01 Venice Map for Lion Boy 2

Medium Pen and ink

Brief Illustrate an aerial view of Venice

Commissioned by Nick Stearn

Client Puffin Books

silver
Christopher Wormell

02 The Big Ugly Monster

Medium	Watercolour
Brief	The big ugly monster (author and illustrator)
Commissioned by	Tom Maschler
Client	Random Century

Christopher Wormell was born in Gainsborough, Lincolnshire, in 1955. On leaving school in 1973 he studied painting with his father, L.J.W. Linsey, while working at numerous temporary or part time jobs.

In 1982, inspired by the work of Thomas Bewick, Reynolds Stone and Charles Tunnicliffe, he took up wood engraving with a view to illustrating books. He became a full time illustrator in 1983 and has since illustrated many books as well as working extensively in the fields of advertising, design and editorial illustration, both in the U.K. and abroad.

In recent years he has begun writing and illustrating children's picture books as for example, "Two Frogs" for which he won the bronze medal at the 2003 Smarties Prize

Recent work includes: A stamp design for the Royal Mail millennium set, Neighbourhood watch images for the Metropolitan Police Force, numerous package designs for Waitrose and a billboard poster campaign for Adnams beer.

Christopher Wormell lives in London with his wife and three children.

124

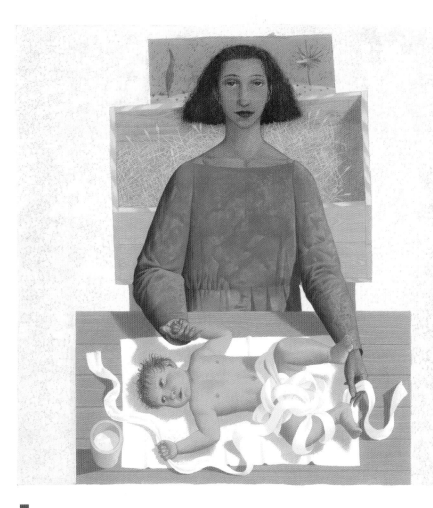

bronze
Peter Malone

03 I am Mother Mary

Medium Gouache

Brief To illustrate a book called 'How Many Miles to Bethlehem' by Kevin Crossley-Holland

Commissioned by Fiona Kennedy

Client Orion Publishing

Peter Malone went to art school at Winchester (foundation) and Coventry (painting). He taught drawing for fifteen years on the foundation course at Bournemouth and to quote him "tried to be an artist the rest of the time with distinctly limited success."

His first job as an illustrator was for Radio Times in 1993. Since then he has continued to work as an illustrator, mostly on children's books for US publishers.

He was born in Hampshire and has lived in both London and Bath since leaving college.

"I was necessarily pretty much self-taught, though I had help from Fig Taylor at the AOI in how to produce and organise a portfolio. I used previously published articles on food, drink and travel from magazines as project briefs to produce my own images. Funnily enough I've rarely been asked to do editorial work on these topics, though the swaddling bands shown here bear a passing resemblance to tagliatelle . The truth will out."

Napoleon was a small brown dog with very big ideas.
One day, while he was out on his boat exploring,
he spotted land through his telescope.
"Perfect!" he said. "My very own paradise island!"

And he rowed ashore.

04

05

Napoleon got very excited.
"I want it to be tall . . .

. . . and wide . . .

. . . with a great ocean view!"

Napoleon had so many ideas that he
scoffed down his dinner as quick as
he could and rushed off in search of

. . . just the right place!

"Why is he in such a hurry?" asked Crab.
"No idea," said Bunny.
"Never mind," said Bear. "Let's play!"

Adria Meserve

04 'Napoleon Rows Ashore'

Medium Mixed media

Brief To write and illustrate a full colour picture book.
The story is about Napoleon, a small brown dog with
very big ideas

Commissioned by Natasha Biebow, Senior Commissioning Editor

Client The Bodley Head - Random House Children's Books

Adria Meserve

05 'Napoleon's Big Idea'

Medium Mixed media

Brief Double-page spread showing Napoleon getting carried
away with his ideas for a new island home

Commissioned by Natasha Biebow, Senior Commissioning Editor

Client The Bodley Head - Random House Children's Books

Ian Benfold Haywood

06 Usborne Book of Christmas Stories
Medium Pen and ink
Brief Chapter heading illustrations
Commissioned by Mary Cartwright
Client Usborne Publishing Ltd

07

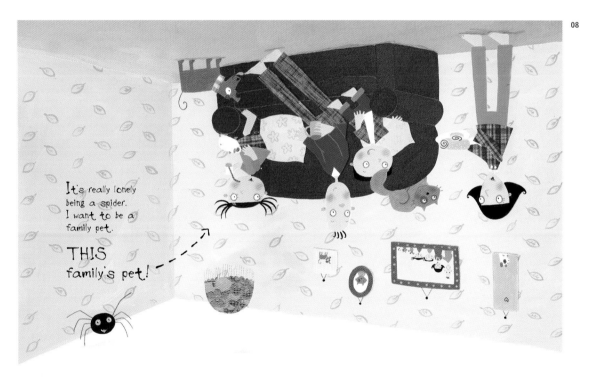

08

Images 29 **Children's Books**

Lydia Monks

07 Aaarrgghh, Spider, Cover

Medium Mixed media

Brief To create an eye-catching cover that would portray a
weary relationship between a spider and a family

Commissioned by Susan Rueben

Client Egmont

Lydia Monks

08 Aaarrgghh, Spider, Family

Medium Mixed media

Brief The spider is telling the story in this spread. Therefore,
we see him the right way up, and everyone else is
upside down

Commissioned by Susan Rueben

Client Egmont

Emily Windsnap and the Monster from the Deep

Liz Kessler

09

Sarah Gibb

09 Emily Windsnap & the Monster from the Deep

Medium Watercolour

Brief artwork: Emily Windsnap & the Monster from the Deep

Commissioned by Jane Hughes

Client Orion Children's Publishing

10

Stephen Waterhouse

10   I Started my Journey from the South Pole

Medium   Acrylic

Brief   To write and illustrate the third book in the 'Get Busy'
series about a penguin family

Commissioned by   Emma Matthewson

Client   Bloomsbury Children's Books

12

11

Measle Stubbs is not a boy known for his good luck. He's thin and weedy and hasn't had a bath for years. Not only that but he has to live in a horrible old house with his horrible old guardian, Basil Tramplebone.

And then, just when Measle thinks things can't get any worse, he's zapped by one of Basil's evil spells. Now he's only a few centimetres tall and trapped in the world of a toy train set. It's times like these when you could do with a few friends to help you out.

Measle needs to be more than just a smelly little orphan — he needs to be a hero and come up with a plan . . . quick!

Cover illustration by Chris Mould
ISBN 0-19-271952-1

OXFORD
UNIVERSITY PRESS

www.oup.com

9 780192 719522
£8.99 RRP

MEASLE AND THE WRATHMONK

IAN OGILVY

OXFORD

MEASLE AND THE WRATHMONK

IAN OGILVY

A small boy, a big adventure, and one **enormous** cockroach . . .

Chris Mould

11 Measle and the Wrathmonk

Medium Pen and ink (line and tone)

Brief Measle and the Wrathmonk: open brief for a cover illustration

Commissioned by Jo Cameron / Liz Cross

Client Oxford University Press

Chris Mould

12 Measle and the Wrathmonk

Medium Pen and ink (line and tone)

Brief Measle and the Wrathmonk: open brief for an illustration of the horrible house as described in the book

Commissioned by Jo Cameron / Liz Cross

Client Oxford University Press

13

Garry Parsons

13 Krong!

Medium Acrylic

Brief An alien has landed in Carl's garden and he only
speaks Gobbledygook! Carl tries out every language
he can think of - can he make contact?

Commissioned by Natasha Biebow

Client Random House Children's Books

David Lucas

14 Old Woman

Medium Ink on wallpaper

Brief Illustration for 'The Ugly Great Giant'
by Malachy Doyle

Commissioned by Nia Roberts

Client Orchard Books

15

16

Images 29 **Children's Books**

Sam Holland

15 I'm Bored on a Journey

Medium Watercolour

Brief To create a family in a variety of situations
corresponding to games/matching humour of the
writing/interior and cover

Commissioned by Rosemary Davidson

Client Bloomsbury Publications

Joy Gosney

16 Al Capone Does My Shirts

Medium Mixed media

Brief Jacket for a novel about the escapades of a group of
children living on the island of Alcatraz when Capone
was incarcerated there

Commissioned by Yeti Mccaldin

Client Bloomsbury PLC

17

18

Sarah Gill

17 Rain Clouds Leaving

Medium Gouache & ink

Brief Double page spread for a picture book about
a rainy day

Commissioned by Anna Milbourne

Client Usborne Publishing Ltd

Sarah Gill

18 Plants and Roots

Medium Gouache & ink

Brief Double page spread for a picture book about
a rainy day

Commissioned by Anna Milbourne

Client Usborne Publishing Ltd

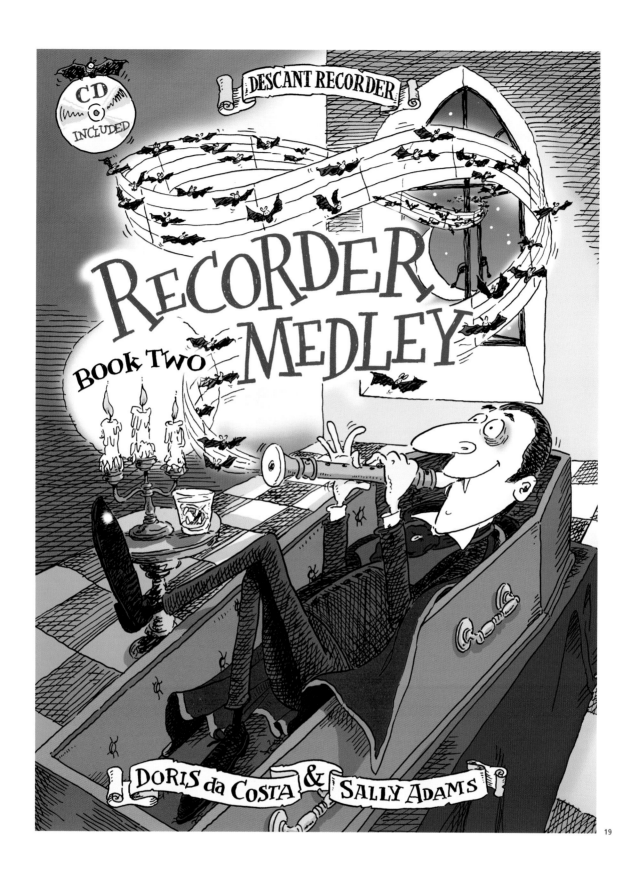

Images 29 **Children's Books**

Andy Hammond

19 Dracula's Dream

Medium   Mixed media

Brief   To design a cover using a song title from the book
which would appeal to children

Commissioned by   Peter Maxwell

Client   Cramer Music Ltd

books

Matt Bookman

Peter Dyer

Geoff Grandfield

Jonny Hannah

Jamie Trendall

William Webb

Gold

Andy Potts

Andy Potts was born in Dudley, England in 1973, with a pencil fused to his hand. He has created images and drawn for as long as he can remember so it seemed inevitable he would end up graduating with BA Hons in Illustration at Portsmouth University in 1995. After Portsmouth he pursued a career in New Media, designing interfaces and motion graphics for PC games, CD-ROM, television and video. Using these digital skills he honed his illustration style for freelance work and forged dual careers while working in Brighton, Winchester and finally London where he now works as Lead Designer at Abbey Road Interactive.

As a freelance illustrator and animator he has worked for high profile advertising, publishing and editorial clients such as TBWA/GTT, Random House, The Guardian and Time Out.

At Abbey Road Interactive he has become one of the leading designer/animators for DVD in the field and has created menu systems for international acts such as Radiohead, Coldplay, U2, New Order and David Bowie.

138

01 The Fruit Palace

Medium Digital

Brief To design a wrap around cover that captured the spirit of this travel book about the Colombian cocaine trade

Commissioned by Eleanor Crow

Client Random House

silver

Andy Bridge

02 Maigret's Little Joke

Medium Collage

Brief Audio CD and cassette cover image of
George Simenon Maigret's stories

Commissioned by Andrew Hall

Client BBC Audiobooks

Graduating from Brighton in 1989, Andy worked from Great Western Studios in West London until August 2004. He has since moved to France where he is continuing his illustration work and also plans to explore other areas of painting.

Much of his work comes from the major editorial and publishing houses in the UK, Europe and US. In 2002, he illustrated the Man Booker Prize winning Life of Pi and in 2004, he was commissioned to produce the cover artwork for Birds without Wings, the follow-on novel to Louis de Bernière's Captain Corelli's Mandolin

Other commissions include shop window displays for fashion designer Anya Hindmarch, artwork for private homes, film sets and cruise ships.

140

Matthew studied Graphic Design at Middlesex Polytechnic, followed by postgraduate study in Illustration at Central St. Martin's. He recently completed an MA in Fine Art at Cardiff University. He has worked for many and varied clients including The London Sinfonietta, Channel 4 Television, Penguin Books, The British Council, The Guardian, The Times, Decca and HMV Music. Alongside commissioned work, Matthew also exhibits his own work which utilises a diverse range of processes such as print, photography, animation, assemblage and digital media. Currently, this work explores and is informed by ideas and myths about social belief, originality and authenticity.

bronze
Matthew Richardson

03	**Love in the Time of Cholera**
Medium	Mixed media
Brief	Illustrate Gabriel García Márquez's 'Love in the Time of Cholera'
Commissioned by	Jon Gray
Client	Penguin Books

04

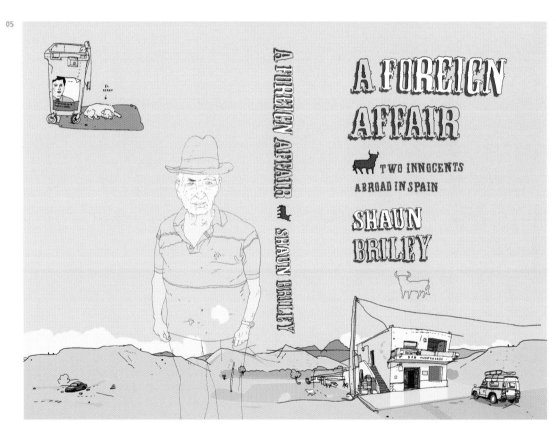

05

Andrew Davidson

04 Welder

Medium Gouache

Brief To create 20 images for the Cunard book of comparisons

Commissioned by Rob Hall

Client The Open Agency

Olivier Kugler

05 A Foreign Affair

Medium Digital

Brief Cover artwork for the book by Shaun Bailey: A Foreign Affair

Commissioned by David Eldridge

Client Two Associates

Harriet Russell

06 The True and Outstanding Adventures of the Hunt Sisters

Medium Silkscreen

Brief Cover with a sense of fun and innocence aimed at women aged 20-40, also reflects that the book is a series of letters

Commissioned by Kari Brownlie

Client Simon & Schuster

The True and Outstanding Adventures of the Hunt Sisters

Elisabeth Robinson

"A story to treasure... I loved it"

ADRIANA TRIGIANI

HOLLYWOOD

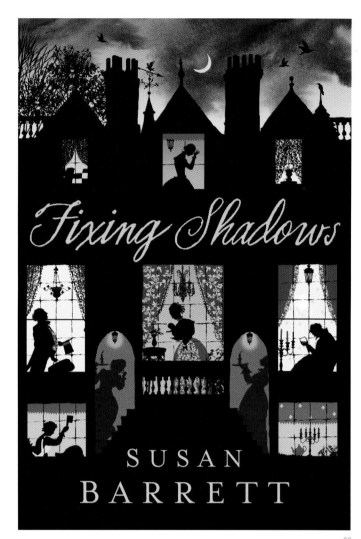

Jackie Parsons

07 Next Stop Hope

Medium Mixed media

Brief Jacket design for a collection of short stories by various writers

Commissioned by Ian Daley

Client Route Publishing

Sarah Gibb

08 Fixing Shadows

Medium Watercolour

Brief Cover artwork for the book Fixing Shadows by Susan Barrett

Commissioned by Ami Smithson

Client Headline

Sarah Perkins

09 Ghost Heart

Medium Mixed media

Brief Illustrate the story of the relationship between two cousins set against the background of the Cuban Revolution

Commissioned by Claire Ward

Client Transworld

10

'Unlike anything anyone else has written ... one of our finest writers still breaking new ground' William Dalrymple, *Observer*

'Fascinating, completely engages the reader' *Daily Mail*

Redmond O'Hanlon has visited the world's most dangerous places, but nothing prepares him for two weeks aboard a deep-sea-fishing trawler in the North Atlantic. Setting out in a hurricane and immediately sick as a dog, finding his sea legs and discovering exactly what kind of disgusting (not to mention explosive) creatures come up from the deep, O'Hanlon bravely tries to become one of the crew. But sleep deprivation, the surreal sea monsters caught in the nets and the increasingly bizarre banter mean that this journey soon becomes a dark – but hilarious – night of the soul ...

'Its pages pitch, roll, sway, heave, surge and yaw. A masterpiece of gonzo naturalism' *Literary Review*

'Remarkable. You would be hard-pushed to find a better analysis of why males do dangerous things and what that does to them. O'Hanlon is the best kind of shipmate: funny, wise, garrulous and generous; his book salted with memorable anecdotes and wit' *Guardian*

'Always compelling ... cleverly worked into the exchanges with the crew is a mounting, on-board paranoia ... that grows more alarming by the hour' *Sunday Times*

'Very funny and touching' *Sunday Telegraph*

read more

ISBN 0-140-27668-8

PENGUIN
Travel
£00.00

9 780140 276688

penguin.com

Illustration by Russell Cobb

'A roller-coaster ride into the heart of Atlantic darkness' Daily Telegraph

Trawler

REDMOND O'HANLON

REDMOND O'HANLON

Images 29 **Books**

Russell Cobb

10 Trawler

Medium Acrylic

Brief Cover image for Redmond O'Hanlon's book 'Trawler' about a journey through the North Atlantic

Commissioned by Andrew Smith

Client Penguin Books

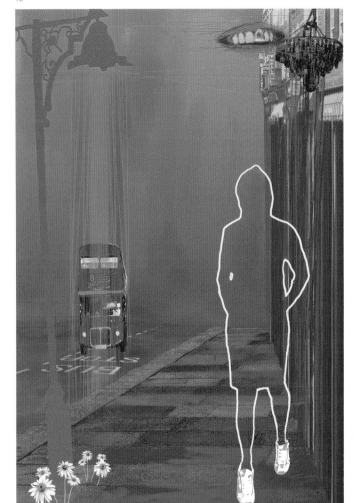

Rowena Dugdale

11 Nature Cure

Medium Digital

Brief A personal story by the author of how his love of
nature and the English countryside helped him to
defeat depression

Commissioned by Eleanor Crow

Client Random House

Marina Caruso

12 Going East

Medium Digital

Brief Book cover: Charting one woman's journey
from a life of privilege to finding peace in London's
gritty East End

Commissioned by Christian Sartorio

Client Edizioni Selecta

Kate Miller

13   Sweetness and Light

Medium   Digital

Brief   Cover for 'Sweetness and Light, the Mysterious History
of the Honey Bee' by Hattie Ellis

Commissioned by   Alice Wright

Client   Hodder & Stoughton

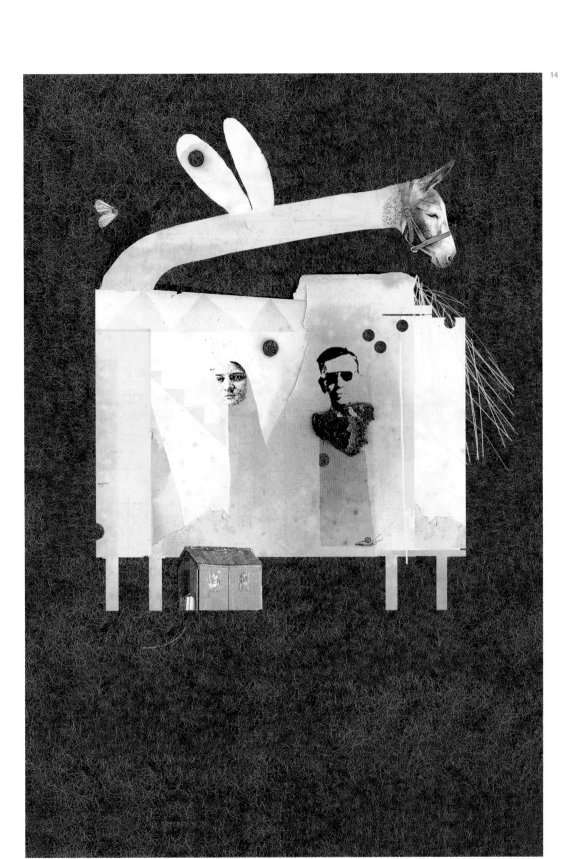

Matthew Richardson

14 One Hundred Years of Solitude

Medium Mixed media

Brief Illustrate Gabriel García Márquez's
'One Hundred Years of Solitude'

Commissioned by Jon Gray

Client Penguin Books

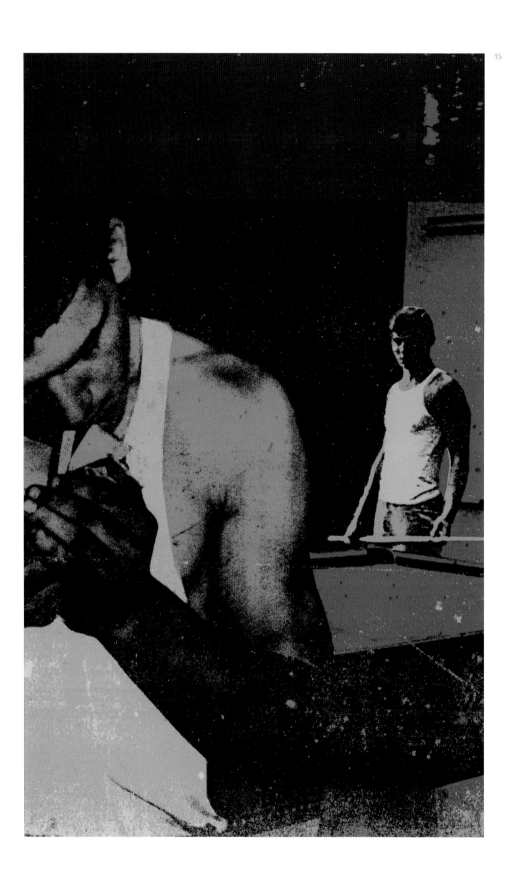

Images 29 **Books**

Alex Williamson

15   Rumblefish

Medium   Digital

Brief   Book cover for SE Hinton novel 'Rumblefish'

Commissioned by   Virri Sheatsley

Client   Random House

student

Greg Clarke
Ben Cox
Dan Fern
Willi Gray
Mike Litherland

Gold

Irfana Biviji

01 **Himalayas**

Medium Gouache

Brief An hypothetical book jacket project in college, designed for subject, expedition to Himalayas

Irfana enrolled on an Applied Art diploma in L.S. Raheja College in Mumbai. She has had early success with her work when she received two awards from her college (Best Portrait and Best Sketch). This made her aware that she had a flair for drawing.

She was determined to develop her talents further and therefore took a big step and came to England to study Illustration at Falmouth College of Arts where she met like-minded illustrators. Irfana took along the colours of busy Bombay streets as her inspiration and her dad encouraged and supported her throughout.

People play an important role in her life and she is always fascinated by human behaviour. Coming to England has made her acutely aware of similarities and differences in the characters and culture of people. While drawing human forms she tries to catch expressions and emotions through the medium that she is using.

She is highly inspired by the illustrations of Finn Campbell-Notman, E.H Shepard and Arthur Rackham.

152

silver
Swava Harasymowicz

02 **Hell**

Medium Mixed media

Brief Illustration for H. Andersen's 'The Girl Who Trod on the Loaf' - about a girl sent to hell to act as a living statue for ever

Swava was born in Poland in 1970 and graduated from Jagiellonian University in Krakow with an MA in English Philology. She then worked as a freelance translator for several years before moving to London in 1998. In July 2004, she graduated from Middlesex University with a BA in Illustration, and in September 2004 she started an MA Communication Art and Design at the Royal College of Art.

All of her work is drawing based. She enjoys fast line drawing, screen print, linocut, painting, collage with PhotoShop manipulation… and sees herself as a visual artist whose work can be used in many areas.

Her inspiration comes from nature, space, unknown places, movement, literature, surreal humour, history, and good films.

Early awards include 1st prize at WPP Atticus magazine cover design competition 2004 – 1st prize Uniqlo t-shirt design competition 2005 edition – and the SAA Poster Competition 2004 'Eating Out in London'.

154

bronze
Richard Merritt

03   **'The Kremlinaires'**

Medium   Digital / ink

Brief   To design and illustrate a poster for the
Russian band 'The Kremlinaires'

Born in 1982 and from Enfield,
North London, Richard Merritt
studied art and design foundation
at Central Saint Martins College of
Art, before going on to gain a BA
(Hons) degree in illustration at
Kingston University, Surrey -
graduating in 2004. During his
time there, his work was selected
for Kingston Museum's Brill
Heritage Collection, which now
appears in a published book of the
collection. He was also twice
commended in consecutive
competitions for the Fine Press
Book Association. He has worked
on numerous private commissions,
including a portrait of the Mayor
of Enfield, and is currently a
practising illlustrator, having been
invited to join the illustration
agency "The Organisation" after
his degree show.

Yumi Okuda

04 Warfare

Medium Mixed media

Brief To illustrate an editorial piece about food for journalists reporting from Baghdad

Richard Merritt

05 One Man and His Cock

Medium Digital / ink

Brief To design and illustrate a fable, which is to be presented as a book of 16 double page spreads

Client Fine Press Book Association

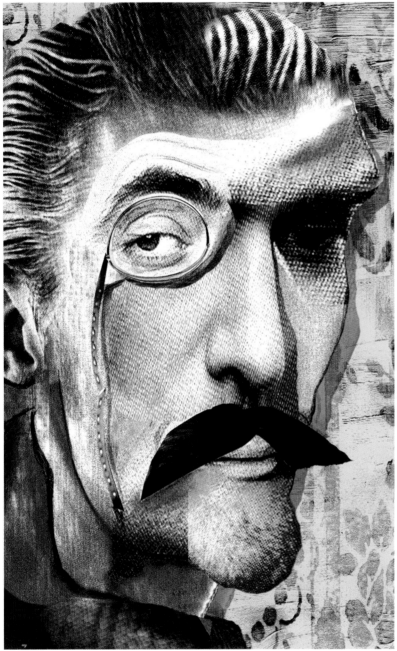

Jo Shuttleworth

06 The Loved One

Medium Collage

Brief To produce a book cover for 'The Loved One' by
Evelyn Waugh

Jo Shuttleworth

07 Things Our Mothers Taught Us

Medium Collage

Brief Produce an image for a women's magazine article
about how a mother teaches her child to bake

08

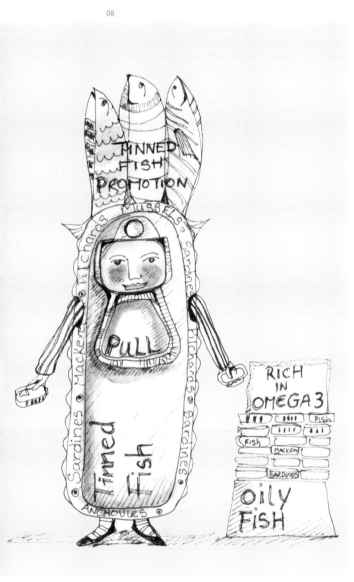

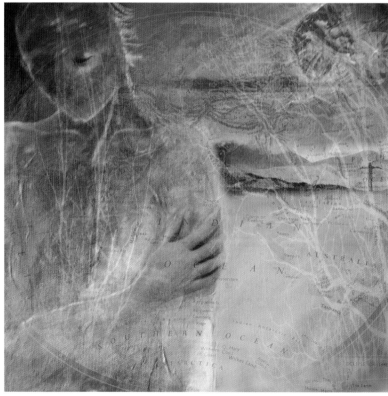

09

10

Pamela Gray

08 Tinned Fish

Medium Mixed media

Brief Accompanying illustration for a magazine article
promoting the benefits of oily fish. A nutritious and
often over looked food. University project

Yvonne Lee

09 Acquainted with the Night

Medium Mixed media / Digital

Brief An image inspired by the Robert Frost poem
'Acquainted with the Night'

Yvonne Lee

10 Across Dark Hills

Medium Mixed media / Digital

Brief An image inspired by the Carol Ann Duffy poem
'Words, Wide Night'

Emma Dibben

11 Havana

Medium Mixed media / digital

Brief Visually exploring Havana after a trip to Cuba

Sam McCullen

12 Billy Back-To-Front

Medium Mixed media, digital

Brief A picture book about a back to front boy who learns
that it's good to stand out from the crowd

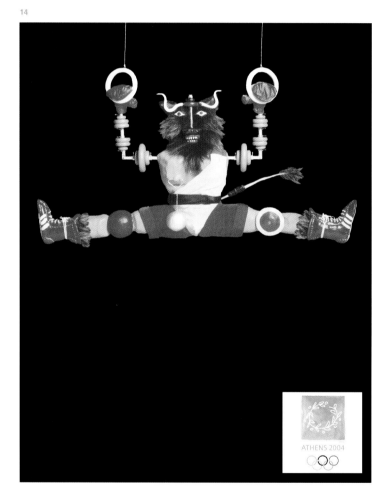

ATHENS 2004

Images 29 **Student**

Fiona Maund

13 Transport for London - Open Spaces

Medium Acrylic & digital

Brief Create a poster to encourage Londoners to visit open
spaces by public transport

Dean Williams

14 Olympics 2004

Medium 3 dimensional / mixed media

Brief Advertise the Olympic Games in Athens 2004 with
mythological Greek folklore

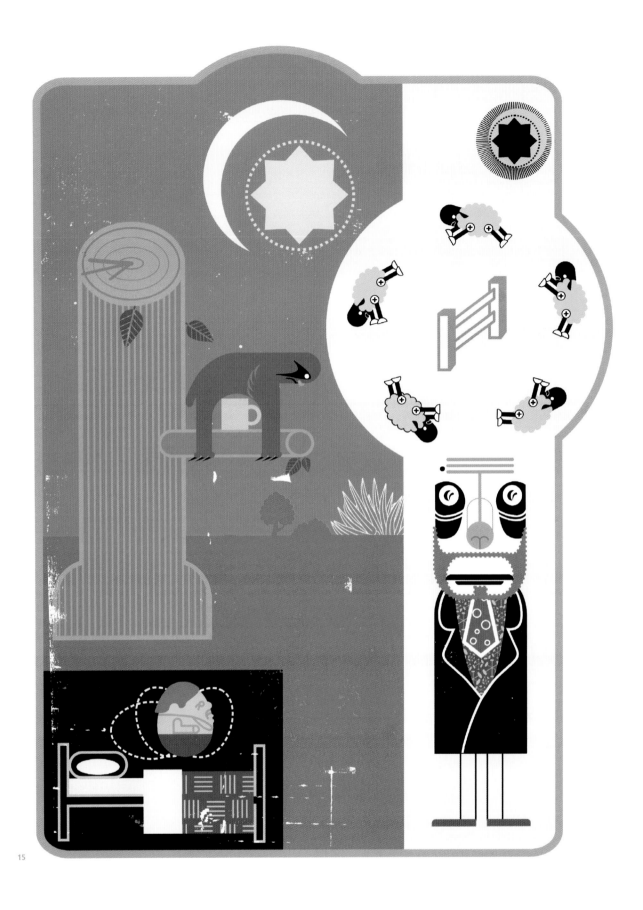

Johnathon Grimwood

15 Insomnia

Medium Digital

Brief Illustrate insomnia conceptually

17

Images 29 **Student**

Laura Scott

16 Objets D'Art (Mann 5a and 5b)

Medium Mixed media

Brief To illustrate a collection of short stories by Thomas
Mann for possible use as book jackets

Laura Scott

17 The Beautiful Boy (Mann 7a and 7b)

Medium Mixed media

Brief To illustrate a collection of short stories by Thomas
Mann for possible use as book jackets

18

19

Rob Flowers

18 Spring Heeled Jack 1

Medium Mixed media

Brief Bring the true legend of Spring Heeled Jack back to
life in an illustrated tale

Rob Flowers

19 Spring Heeled Jack 2

Medium Mixed media

Brief Bring the true legend of Spring Heeled Jack back to
life in an illustrated tale

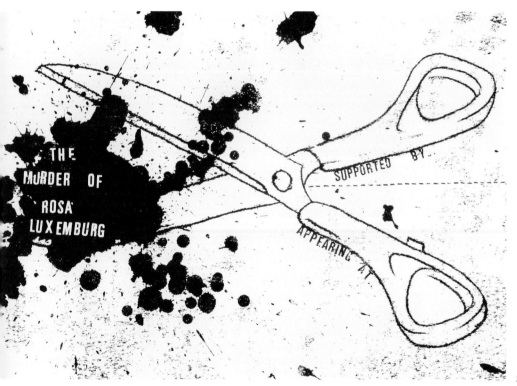

20

21

22

Images 29 **Student**

Harvey

20 Why I Love Porter

Medium Mixed media

Brief University project to illustrate The Guardian article
'Why I Love Porter' using the Cockney rhyming slang
'Elephant's trunk...'

Harvey

21 The Definition of Funny

Medium Mixed media

Brief Illustrate 'funny'

Harvey

22 The Murder of Rosa Luxemburg

Medium Mixed media / screen print

Brief A poster to promote the band
'The Murder of Rosa Luxemburg'

23

24

Hannah McVicar

23 West Side Story

Medium Screen-print

Brief An image which could be used on a poster
for West Side Story

Hannah McVicar

24 Herbal Tea Time

Medium Aqua-tint

Brief An image for front cover of the book: Herbal Tea Time

Images 29 **Student**

Tom Gaul

25 Knockout

Medium Mixed media

Brief To produce an image based on the life of Daniel
Mendoza, the pioneer of technical boxing

Ben McLeod

26 Decade Blending

Medium Mixed media

Brief The blending of clothing from two or more decades to
create one's own unique style

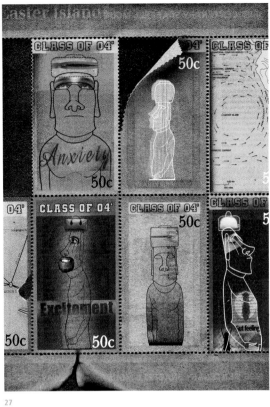

27

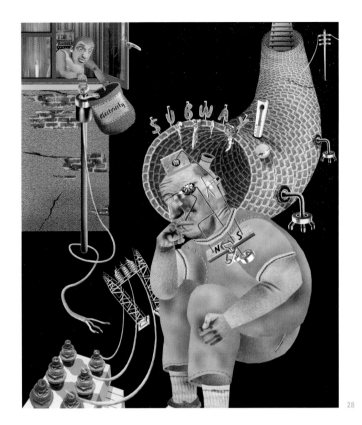

28

29

167

Chintu Shah

27 Easter Island Stamps

Medium Digital

Brief Produce an image in response to the theme 'Let's face it'

Chintu Shah

28 Blackout

Medium Digital

Brief Produce an illustration that can accompany an editorial about how increasingly dependant modern cities are on electricity, following recent blackouts in New York city

Chintu Shah

29 Mechanical Santa

Medium Digital

Brief Produce a Christmas card which can be purchased by university departments to send to associates in the education, commercial and industrial sectors and overseas

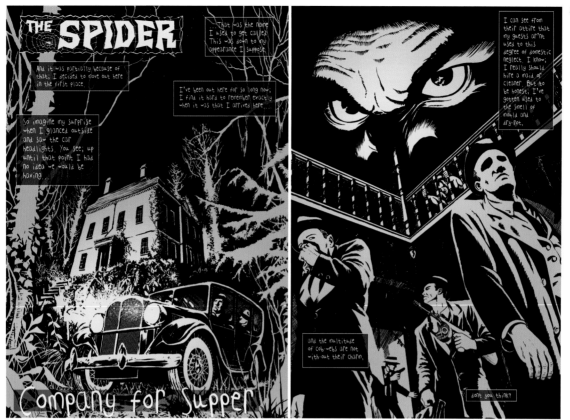

James Fletcher

30   The Spider

Medium   Mixed media

Brief   To utilise illustrated film noir techniques for a magazine story using black & white and no more than two other colours

Paddy Molloy

31   The Bull's Dead - Lets Get it

Medium   Pencil drawing composed digitally

Brief   One of a series of images based on the attitudes towards animals in Spain

32

Andy Davies

32 Little Red Cap

Medium Mixed media

Brief Illustrate the Grimm Brothers tale, 'Little Red Cap'

Philip Grisewood

33 Untitled

Medium Mixed media

Brief This piece was taken from a series of illustrations inspired by George Orwell's novel '1984'

34

Images 29 **Student**

Mayko Fry

34 The Dark Forest

Medium Mixed media

Brief A full page illustration for 'Silence - A Fable' by Edgar
Allan Poe. The demon speaks of a boundary of a
region in Libya

Mayko Fry

35 Desolation

Medium Mixed media

Brief A full page illustration for 'Silence - A Fable' by Edgar
Allan Poe. A demon has found the letters 'desolation'
being written on a rock

Mayko Fry

36 The Demon Touches My Head

Medium Mixed media

Brief A full page illustration for 'Silence - A Fable' by Edgar
Allan Poe. The demon starts telling the narrator a
story about the region

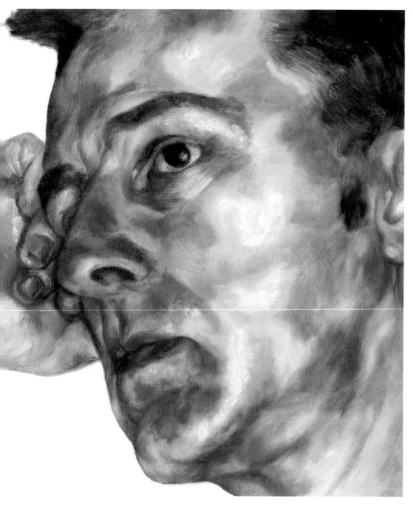

Images 29 **Student**

Jade Perry

37 Untitled

Medium Oils

Brief One of nine paintings which explore voyeurism, cropping and the human form

Jade Perry

38 Untitled

Medium Mixed media

Brief Modern women and their daily rituals with focus on washing and drying oneself

Daniel Thompson

39 Wartime Memories (Evacuees)

Medium Digital

Brief Illustrations based on a story of my grandfather's memories and experiences of growing up during World War II in Coventry

Daniel Thompson

40 Wartime Memories (Air raid)

Medium Digital

Brief Illustrations based on a story of my grandfather's memories and experiences of growing up during World War II in Coventry

41

42

Images 29 **Student**

Caroline Parkinson

41 Carnosaurus

Medium Watercolour

Brief As a self promotional exercise, produce a guide to the
dinosaurs of The Natural History Museum, London

Rosie Scott

42 The Panther Sale

Medium Mixed media

Brief Front cover image for a children's book about a girl
and a very hungry big panther

43

44

Neil Cunningham

43 World Heavyweight Greats - Joe Louis

Medium Mixed media / digital

Brief To produce a series of postcards illustrating the greatest heavyweight boxers of all time

Martyn Shouler

44 Neurosis

Medium Mixed media

Brief Personal experiment. One of a series generated from listening to several conversations at once

45

46

what's a sex toy?

Paul Smith

45 The child born on the Sabbath Day is bonny, blithe, good and gay

Medium Mixed media

Brief To create my own interpretation of the above phrase

Delphine Lebourgeois

46 Sex Toy

Medium Mixed media

Brief One of a series of illustrations on the embarrassing / difficult questions that our children ask us

John Adam Scarratt

47 Parents under Fire

Medium Mixed media

Brief Article on domestic violence by children against
their parents

Fiona Sansom

48 Lose Yourself in a Good Book

Medium Mixed media

Brief Promote reading with the quote 'Lose yourself in a
good book'

Images 29 **Student**

Mary Kilvert

49 Bedtime Stories

Medium Pen & digital

Brief To illustrate an article about bedtime stories

unpublished

Simon Carbery

Tony Chambers

Jonathan Cusick

Nick Hardcastle

Sue Vago

01 **The Drawing Works**

Medium Acrylic

Brief To produce a series of collect and keep
postcards. No 28 based on the theme of
drawing

Russell Cobb

Gold

Russell Cobb trained at Central St.
Martins School of Art in London and
at the Hochschule für Gestaltung
und Kunst Luzern in Switzerland.
After living in Italy and Switzerland
Russell is now based in London and
works from his studio in
Hertfordshire.

Russell has received many industry
plaudits, including 5 Association of
Illustrators Best of British Gold
awards, and in 2003 the
Independent national newspaper
voted him one of Britain's top
ten illustrators.

Russell's work has been featured in
many publications, most recently
3x3 magazine New York, the
international magazine for
contemporary illustration. He now
has an extensive client list
throughout Europe and the USA
and has worked for many leading
art directors in every field of the
illustration industry.

Russell has always paid great
attention to his personal and self-
promotion work, and believes that
constantly exploring new ideas
keeps his commissioned work vital,
fresh and original.

Russell has taught at many
educational establishments
throughout the UK and regularly
returns to teach in Switzerland.

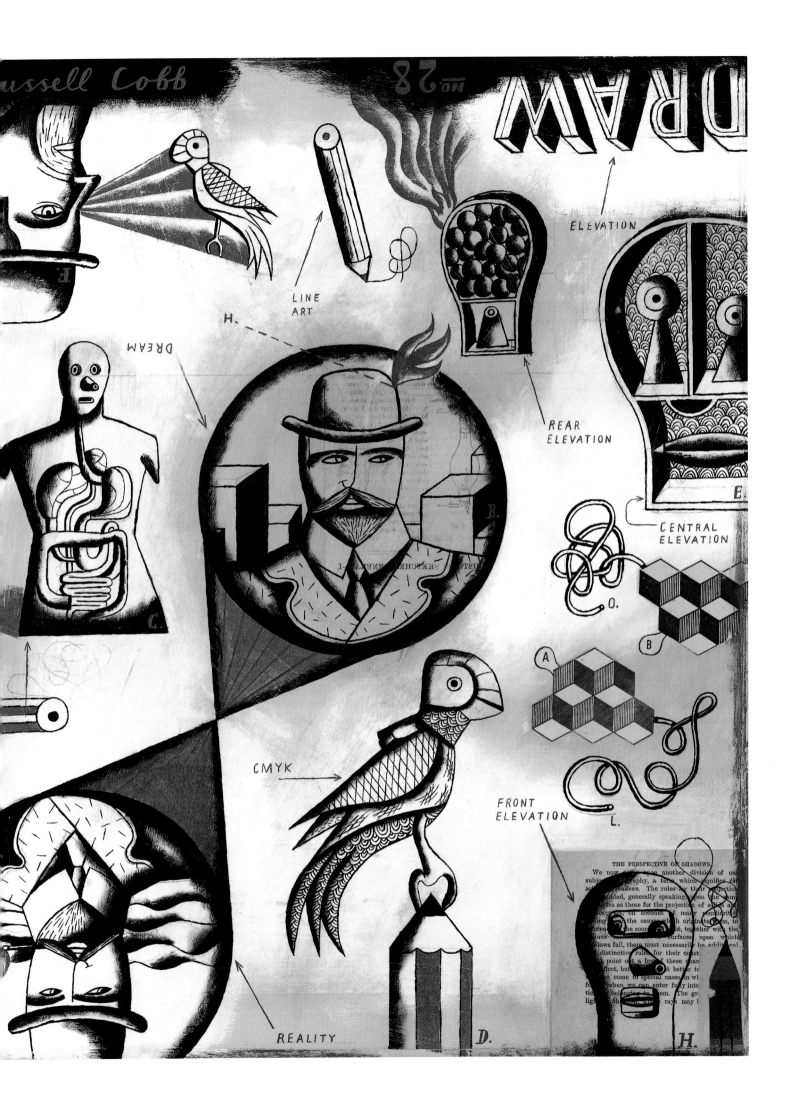

silver

Brian Grimwood

02 **London Zoo**
Medium   Mixed media
Brief   A witty poster for London Zoo

Brian Grimwood has been credited by Print Magazine as having changed the look of British Illustration. He has worked for most of the popular magazines world wide, and has become one of Europe's most innovative and influential illustrators.

In 1983 he founded The Central Illustration Agency and more recently opened a multimedia agency representing new illustrators and animators, CIIA.

CIA and CIIA represent 70 of the world's most prestigious illustrators.

182

Tim has been working as an illustrator for the last fourteen years. In the last eight years he has concentrated solely on children's books, particularly in the 8-12 year old market.

He considers himself lucky to have worked for some of today's best children's writers, including books by Diana Wynne Jones, Gillian Cross, and Adele Geras, Anthony Horrowitz and Aiden Chambers.

Tim's style reflects his love of classic fairy tales and their illustrators.

Tim graduated with a BA Hons Illustration from Camberwell College of Arts and his work has been previously selected in Images 20, Images 22, and Images 26

bronze
Tim Stevens

03 The Snow Queen

Medium Pen and ink (line and wash)

Brief The old woman locked the door. 'I have long wanted
a little girl like you'... For the old lady was an
enchantress - Andersen

04

05

Russell Cobb

04   Writers Block

Medium   Acrylic

Brief   One of a series of illustrated stories depicting a more
personal take on the up and down journey of a
creative life

Russell Cobb

05   The Science Works

Medium   Acrylic

Brief   To produce a series of collect and keep postcards.
No 26 based on the theme of science

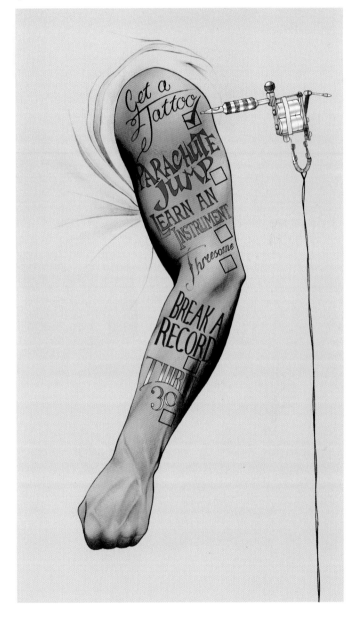

Russell Cobb

06   The Exploration Works

Medium   Acrylic

Brief   To produce a series of collect and keep postcards.
No 25 based on the theme of exploration

David Lynch

07   Things to do Before You're 30

Medium   Digital

Brief   Exploring the essential activities to enjoy before you
reach the magic age of thirty

09

10

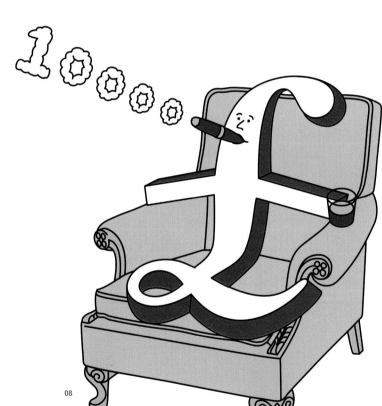

08

Cyrus Deboo

08   Wealthy Pound

Medium   Digital

Brief   Self promotion: Wealthy Pound

Cyrus Deboo

09   New Year 2004

Medium   Digital

Brief   Self promotion: New Year 2004

Cyrus Deboo

10   Love You Loads

Medium   Digital

Brief   Self promotion: Love You Loads

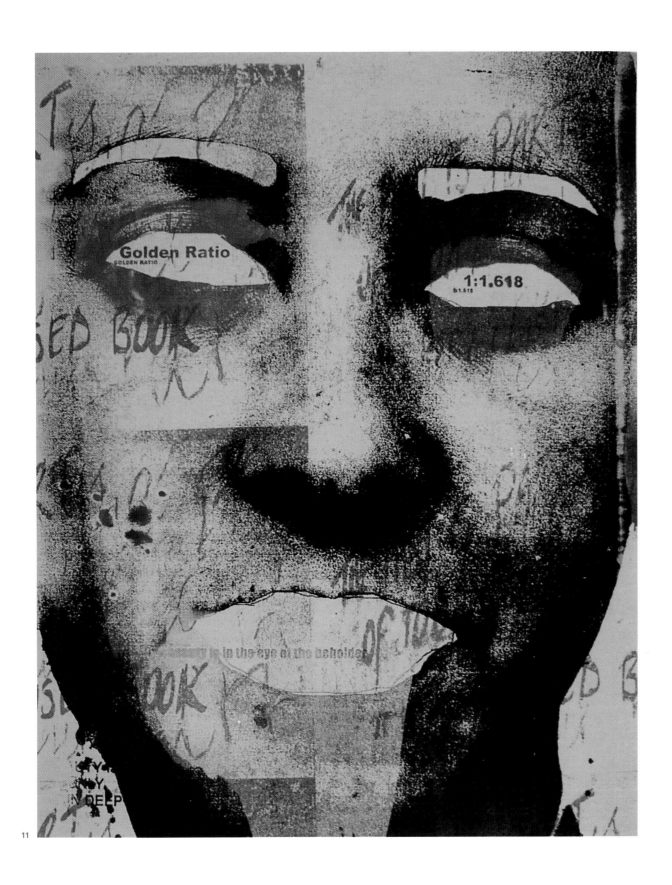

Tara Coles

11 Beauty is in the Eye of the Beholder

Medium Mixed media

Brief Perfection found within nature, specifically looking at
the human face in a mathematical way

12

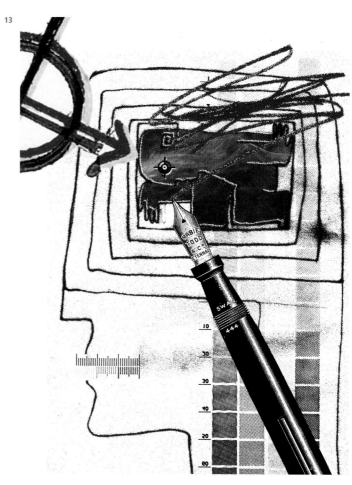

13

188   Images 29 **Unpublished**

Willi Gray

12   Bear to Market

Medium   Drawing & digital collage

Brief   Comment on the less than smooth operations of the
financial world

Willi Gray

13   Frustration

Medium   Drawing & digital collage

Brief   The frustration experienced when the images on paper
fail to match up to the ideas in your head

Imogen Slater

14 Doggy Style

Medium Digital

Brief Personal, experimental work

Images 29 **Unpublished**

Lorna Siviter

15 No More Daddy

Medium Digital

Brief A day at the races is proving not much fun for little Timmy

Emilia Brumini

16 Harmonica Player

Medium Mixed media

Brief The harmonica player is an inspiration for a study of white on black, mixing pastel and gouache, adding a subtle red colour. Self promotional work

Nathan Fletcher

17 House Burglar

Medium Mixed media digital

Brief Image of a house burglar - self promotion

Mick Marston

18 Nuts

Medium Mixed media

Brief Nuts: The English language can have the same word
meaning totally different things, confusing for those
attempting to learn it

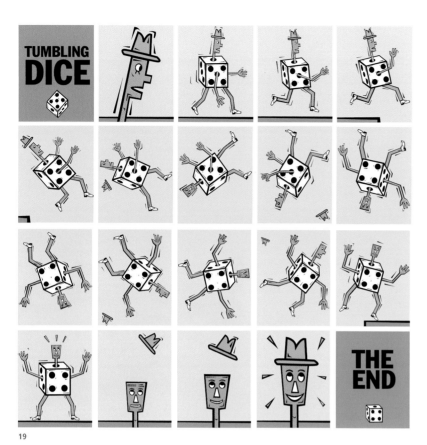

19

20

Images 29 **Unpublished**

Patrick MacAllister

19 Tumbling Dice

Medium Digital

Brief Promotional flip book

Daren Mason

20 Coffin Mouth

Medium Mixed media

Brief To illustrate a quote 'We are digging our own grave with our teeth' Thomas Moffat 17th Century

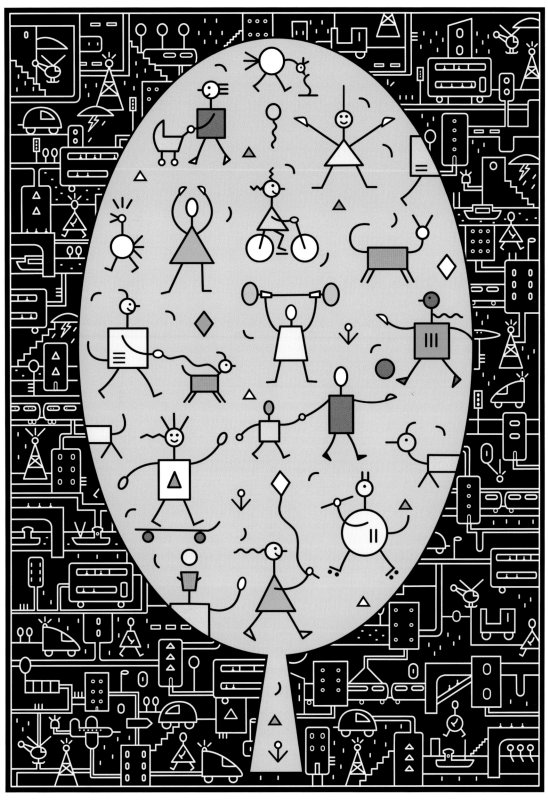

Patrick MacAllister

21 Open Space

Medium Digital

Brief To produce an artwork suitable for use as a poster for
Transport for London

Images 29 **Unpublished**

Janet Woolley

22 Frog Prince 1

Medium Mixed media

Brief Cover for a series of samples for
'The Frog Prince' re-written

Janet Woolley

23 Frog Prince 2

Medium Mixed media

Brief Inside illustration - part of series of samples for
'The Frog Prince' re-written

24

Carol Seatory

24 Mermaid in Bath

Medium Ink & digital

Brief Self promotional

Images 29 **Unpublished**

Stephen Collins

25 John Prescott

Medium Mixed media & Photoshop

Brief Self-promotion for contemporary style of caricature

Stephen Collins

26 Patrick Moore

Medium Mixed media & Photoshop

Brief Self-promotion for contemporary style of caricature

27

28

Stephen Collins

27 Kate Moss

Medium Mixed media & Photoshop

Brief Self-promotion for contemporary style of caricature

Ric Machin

28 Sarah

Medium Oils

Brief Self promotional work. Tenth in the series of this subject; one a year is produced

29

30

Images 29 **Unpublished**

Giulio Iurissevich

29 Break Dance

Medium Digital

Brief Self promotion

Vault49

30 Untitled

Medium Digital

Brief Collaboration between Vault49 and photographer
Stephan Langmanis

Paul Thurlby

31 Schumachine

Medium Mixed media

Brief Portrait of Michael Schumacher

32

33

Images 29 **Unpublished**

Paquebot

32　She Likes You

Medium　Mixed media

Brief　In life, it is equally vital that you get on well with your
friends' pets

Paquebot

33　Can Can

Medium　Mixed media

Brief　Portray a gentleman's night out in Paris ca. 1900

Paquebot

34　Yellow Pencil Cab

Medium　Mixed media

Brief　Create a New York scene with a pencil

35

Images 29 **Unpublished**

Paquebot

35 Are You Looking After Your Savings?

Medium Mixed media

Brief Your savings can be eroded while you are
not aware of it

Paquebot

36 The Boss

Medium Mixed media

Brief Portrait of a boss who exploits his staff and
abuses his position

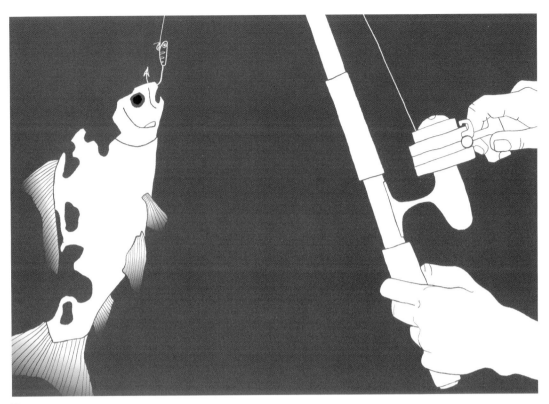

37

38

Emma Peascod

37 Fishing for Koi (Bad Karma)

Medium Mixed media

Brief Illustrate the idea: what goes around comes around

Nick Reddyhoff

38 King of Cool

Medium Digital

Brief Homage to Steve McQueen

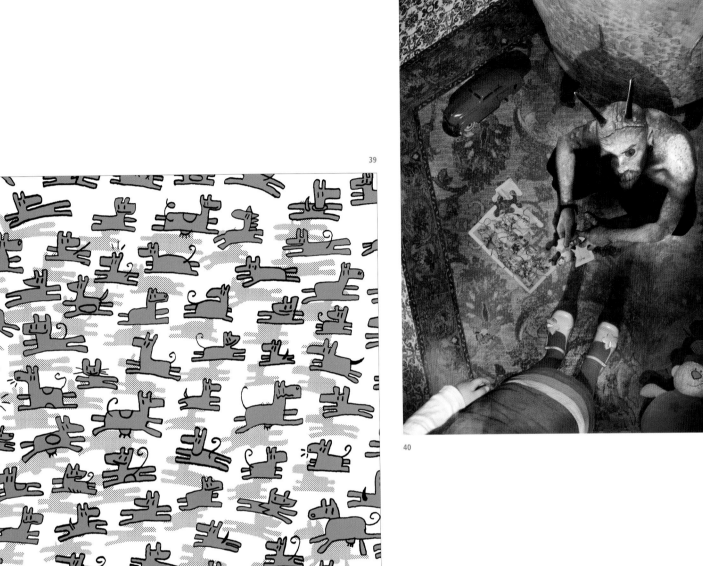

39

40

Images 29 **Unpublished**

Dominic Trevett

39 Running Animals

Medium Digital

Brief What happens if you get many animals, put them in a
confined space and then allow them to run?

Darren Hopes

40 Charlotte's New Friend

Medium Mixed media

Brief My evil twin - just because something looks
unpleasant it does not mean that it is

Ray Nicklin

41 Two Views, One Landscape

Medium Digital

Brief Collaboration - bringing together two types of
thinking. A proposition for the cover of an illustration
agency annual

Pablo Bernasconi

42 Star Fisher

Medium Collage

Brief The Star Fisher looks for someone with a
lot of imagination

43

44

Images 29 **Unpublished**

Daniela Jaglenka Terrazzini

43 Eel Goes to the Fortune Teller

Medium Mixed media

Brief Personal work illustrating 'The Snag' by Ted Hughes

Daniela Jaglenka Terrazzini

44 Heron's Long Bill

Medium Mixed media

Brief Personal work illustrating 'The Snag' by Ted Hughes

45

Daniela Jaglenka Terrazzini

45   Lily in the Mirror

Medium   Mixed media

Brief   Personal work: Lily and Bert

Julia Camden

46   Green Pound

Medium   Mixed media

Brief   Illustrate an article about the dilemma of
ethical investment

47

Images 29 **Unpublished**

Paul Burgess

47 Jazz

Medium Mixed media

Brief Personal piece of work produced for an exhibition on the theme of music/culture

Paul Burgess

48 Red Girls

Medium Mixed media

Brief Experimental piece of work produced for fashion company 'Simultane' in Brighton

Images 29 **Unpublished**

Lasse Skarbovik

49 Health

Medium Digital

Brief Unpublished illustration for a health magazine about
saving money in the health market

Commissioned by Doug Ponte

Client Health Leaders Magazine

Scott Chambers

50 Brind & the Dogs of War

Medium Mixed media

Brief Children's book cover age 9+, jumping dog being held
back by his boy companion minutes before being
released and ready to attack

Commissioned by Jaqui McDonough

Client Puffin Books

51

52

Victoria Bodycote

51 Davy Drives a Dragon

Medium Mixed media

Brief Illustrate a rhyme about a boy who dreamt he
drove a dragon

Patrick Farncombe

52 Blink

Medium Digital

Brief Self portrait

Images 29 **Unpublished**

Rian Hughes

53 A Message for the Voices of Youth

Medium Digital

Brief A comment on the way certain 'musikal artistz' mangle the English language

Rian Hughes

54 Autumn Girl

Medium Digital

Brief Series of greetings cards for the 'boutique' card market, illustrating different moods and characters

55

56

Nathan Daniels

55 Shotgun Funeral

Medium Digital

Brief Man, who's will states that his ashes be loaded into shotgun shells and fired in his favourite places

Jasmine Chin

56 Terror is the Best Remedy for Phobias

Medium Mixed media

Brief Treat peoples phobias quicker by giving a drug that makes them more fearful, followed by continuous exposure to what they dread

57

58

59

Images 29 **Unpublished**

Adrian B McMurchie

57 Top of the Town

Medium Watercolour

Brief Piece for stationery. The aim being to express the dynamic contours of city buildings and reflect the vigour of urban life

Elly Walton

58 Interview Techniques

Medium Digital

Brief Self-promotional editorial piece based on an amusing article about bad interview techniques

Dominic Turnbull

59 Chillin'!

Medium Pencil

Brief Self-motivated brief to illustrate the effect of artificial light on a liquid, glass and an aluminium can using pencil only

Michael Bishop

60 Liquid Assets

Medium Acrylic on canvas

Brief Personal project painting figures in interiors

62

Happy
Year
of the
Monkey!

The
nature
of
Monkey is...
IRREPRESSIBLE!

五福 壽富康寧 攸好德 考終命

Images 29 Unpublished

Paul Bommer

61 Absinthe Friends

Medium Digital

Brief A self promotional Bastille Day greeting card

Paul Bommer

62 Year of the Monkey

Medium Digital

Brief A self promotional Chinese New Year greeting card

Paul Bommer

63 Trick Or Treat?

Medium Digital

Brief A self promotional Halloween greeting card

Jan Bowman

64 Rainbow Room, Rockefeller Center

Medium Digital

Brief Drawing from life

Let us go, through certain half-deserted streets,

Images 29 **Unpublished**

Michael Bramman

65 The Pennsylvania Academy Revisited

Medium Digital

Brief Divertissement

Wendy Jones

66 Half Deserted Streets

Medium Digital

Brief Illustrate T.S. Eliot poem: The Lovesong
of J. Alfred Prufrock

67

Mark Harfield

67 Eye on the Ball

Medium Mixed media

Brief Create an image for general world
wide self promotion

68

69

Images 29 **Unpublished**

Rachel Pearce

68 Greda and the Globe

Medium Acrylic

Brief Using the giant globe, the kind and clever princess
showed brave little Greda how to get to the Snow
Queen's palace

Paul Keysell

69 'Robin Goodfellow', A Puck

Medium Mixed media

Brief From an ongoing series of images exploring the work
of William Shakespeare

Alexandra Merry

70 Beach

Medium Mixed media

Brief Self promotional work: Beach

Alexandra Merry

71 Croquet

Medium Mixed media

Brief Funny English Traditions: Croquet

72

73

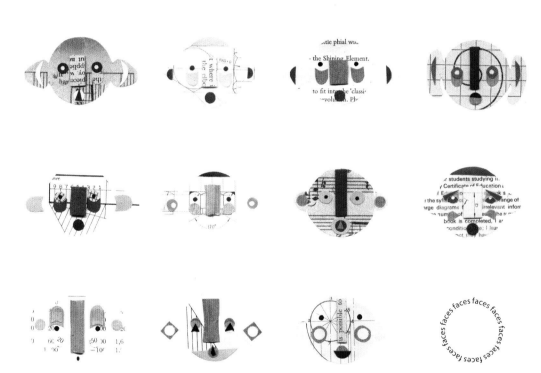

Images 29 **Unpublished**

Victoria Rose

72 Abilities

Medium Litho print

Brief A promotional piece illustrating the word abilities: being able (to do), cleverness, talent, power

Victoria Rose

73 Faces

Medium Collage

Brief A self initiated poster for a recruitment agency

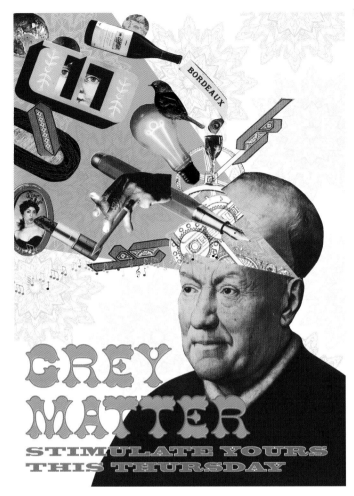

Victoria Rose

74 Grey Matter

Medium Collage

Brief To design an in house poster for a learning and
development day at Grey London

Charlie Fowkes

75 Bubble And Squeak 'Rocket'

Medium Digital

Brief Illustration for a children's book with main characters
'Bubble and Squeak'

76

77

Images 29 **Unpublished**

James Fryer

76 Sleaze

Medium Acrylic

Brief Self initiated work for portfolio. British politics has become notoriously sleazy

James Fryer

77 The Unilateral States of America

Medium Acrylic

Brief Self initiated work for portfolio. America's unilateral approach to international affairs

Jonathan Croft

78 Batman and Robin

Medium Mixed media

Brief One of a series about superheroes

79

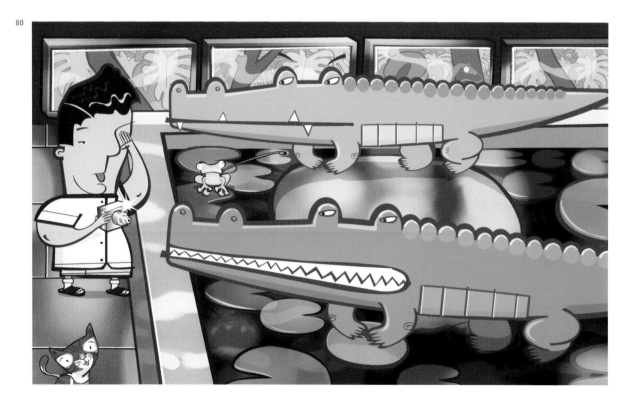

80

Images 29 **Unpublished**

Pete Brewster

79 The Dark Came into the Room Through the
Little Window

Medium Scraperboard

Brief Promotional work illustrating 'The Hobbit' by J.R.R.
Tolkien in a woodcut style

Glyn Brewerton

80 Cat Got Your Tongue

Medium Mixed media / Photoshop

Brief Create an image based on the fact that crocodiles
can't stick out their tongues

Pete Brewster

81 In the End he Poked his Head Through the
Roof of the Trees

Medium Scraperboard

Brief Promotional work illustrating 'The Hobbit' by J.R.R.
Tolkien in a woodcut style

Pete Brewster

82 Now Began the Most Dangerous Part
of all the Journey

Medium Scraperboard

Brief Promotional work illustrating 'The Hobbit' by J.R.R.
Tolkien in a woodcut style

Images 29 **Unpublished**

Sandra Howgate

83 Open Spaces

Medium Digital

Brief Shortlisted for London transport poster competition.
The brief was to show how the humble Travelcard can
get you out and about in London's open spaces.

84

85

Philip Downs

84 Juniper

Medium Acrylic

Brief An illustration for a story based on the medieval concept of the use of Juniper as an abortion drug

Jessica Meserve

85 Sleepy Monkeys

Medium Digital

Brief Character sample for picture book

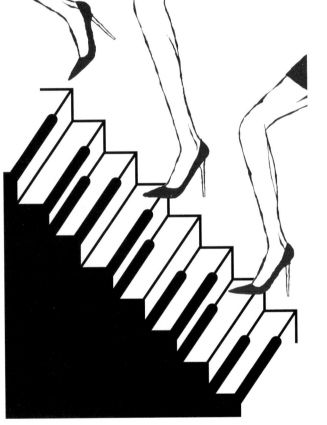

86

Images 29 **Unpublished**

Kenneth Andersson

86 Untitled

Medium Mixed media

Brief Self promotion

Kenneth Andersson

87 Untitled

Medium Mixed media

Brief Self promotion

Kenneth Andersson

88 Untitled

Medium Mixed media

Brief Self promotion

Kenneth Andersson

89 Untitled

Medium Mixed media

Brief Self promotion

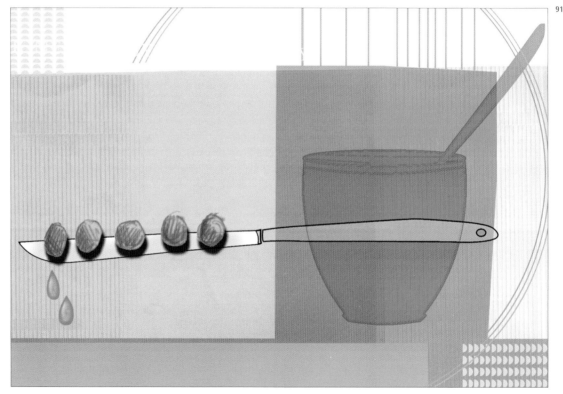

Images 29 **Unpublished**

Beatrice Anna Bona

90 Mother Goose

Medium Watercolour & ink

Brief Mother Goose: Illustration for children's nursery rhyme

Gillian Cook

91 Peas-n-honey

Medium Digital

Brief To illustrate the comic poem 'Peas' by Anon

Fossil Glanville

92 Open Spaces, London by Bus, Tube and River

Medium Digital

Brief To promote London Transport in connection with
London's open spaces

Harriet Russell

93 Star Spotting

Medium Mixed media

Brief Piece for an exhibition on the theme of 'celebrity'

Commissioned by Louisa St Pierre

Client Central Illustration Agency

94

95

Images 29 **Unpublished**

Bev Knowlden

94 Three Men in a Boat

Medium Mixed media

Brief Speculative publishing project for 'Three Men in a
Boat' by Jerome K. Jerome, using traditional model
making combined with digital techniques

Sarah Dyer

95 Open Spaces

Medium Mixed media

Brief To produce a poster for Transport for London
designed to inform all Londoners of the variety of
open spaces in London

William Scott Artus

96 Door Etiquette

Medium Digital

Brief News article on how bouncers are being retrained to
be nicer to customers

97

Images 29 **Unpublished**

Naomi Tipping

97 Migrate to an Open Space

Medium Mixed media

Brief To produce an image for a poster with the theme,
'Open Spaces by Bus, Tube and River'

Sophie Joyce

98 In the Fountain

Medium Digital

Brief This image was inspired by the memories of a trip to
Rome when I was young

Images 29 **Unpublished**

Alan Heighton

99 Table

Medium Digital

Brief A working class tribute to Allen Jones'
famous work 'The Table'

Alan Heighton

100 Park Life

Medium Digital

Brief Strange people gather in a park,
a promotional showcase

Alan Heighton

101 Paper, Scissors

Medium Digital

Brief Self promotional show case of characters
in a park setting

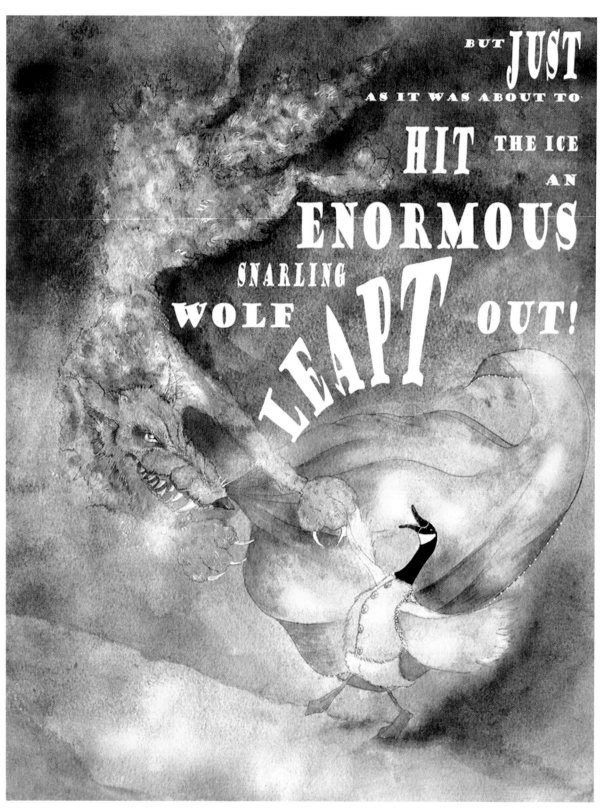

BUT JUST AS IT WAS ABOUT TO HIT THE ICE AN ENORMOUS SNARLING WOLF LEAPT OUT!

102

Images 29 Unpublished

Claire Barker

102 Why Geese Fly South for the Winter

Medium Mixed media

Brief An illustration from 'Why Geese Fly South for the Winter' (author Claire Barker)

Claire Pugh

103 Come Over and Play

Medium Mixed media

Brief Come over and play

Richard Levesley

104 Who's the Veal

Medium Mixed media

Brief Using language that is used within the restaurant to create amusing images

105

106

Images 29 **Unpublished**

Frazer Hudson

105 Island Escape

Medium Digital

Brief Create an illustration to form part of a group
exhibition of postcards entitled 'Summer Confessionals
- what did you do this summer?'

Rebecca Bradley

106 Blues in the Night

Medium Mixed media

Brief Illustrate Johnny Mercer, a Georgia (USA) songwriter's
song 'Blues in the Night'

107

Anna Ildiko Popescu

107 The Elevator

Medium Watercolour & coloured pencils

Brief Illustration for children's counting book. Animals
enter the elevator one by one going to a party on
the roof terrace

108

109

Deborah Stephens

108-109 The Numbers, A Love Story

Medium Mixed media

Brief Children's book. Number 8 and Number 3 fall in love
and decide to add themselves together. But is 8 too
easily divisible for 3?

John & Edward Harrison

110 Dance and Eat Toast

Medium Digital

Brief A postcard from the world of 'what what', an online
world populated with crazy characters

Jacquie O'Neill

111 Call Waiting

Medium Digital

Brief Self promotion: Call waiting

Images 29 **Unpublished**

Philip Wrigglesworth

112 Black Snow

Medium Acrylic

Brief Book cover design for Mikhail Bulgakov's novel
'Black Snow'

Ian Whadcock

113 Facilities Management

Medium Digital

Brief To provide a cover that suggests the answers to all
your facilities management problems are available in
this source book

Commissioned by Jo McEwan

Client McEwan Designs

115

114

John Charlesworth

114 The Revolution will not be Televised

Medium Digital

Brief First in a series of promotional pieces, fusing
the drama of Socialist art with commercial
consumer elements

Paul Brown

115 Therapy

Medium Mixed media

Brief The therapist took my jumbled thoughts and gave
them meaning

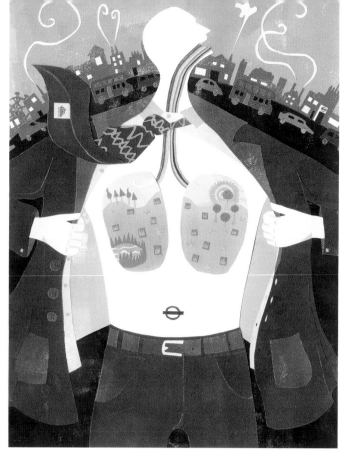

116

117

Images 29 **Unpublished**

Anne Clegg

116 Open Spaces by Bus, Tube and River

Medium Print / collage

Brief Poster campaign to inform all Londoners of the wide
variety of open spaces accessible by Transport for
London networks

Anne Clegg

117 Are You Ready?

Medium Print / collage

Brief To accompany an article in the Times Educational
Supplement about preparing yourself for an interview

Cathy Simpson

118 White Horse Hill

Medium Watercolour

Brief Based on 'White Horse Hill in Uffington'

Bérengère Ducoms

119 Monday Morning

Medium Mixed media

Brief Self-promotion: Calendar page

Air

Fire

Earth

Water

120

121

Images 29 **Unpublished**

Emma Tuzzio

120 The Elements

Medium Acrylic paint

Brief An open response to the four elements of earth, fire, air and water

Andy Potts

121 I'm Drawing Here!

Medium Digital

Brief To create self promotional postcard to advertise my website

Andy Smith

122 The Big Drop

Medium Silkscreen print

Brief The promotion of two self published silkscreen printed books, 'The Big Drop' and 'Lightning Strikes at Fatty's House'

Images 29 **Unpublished**

Stefan Isaacson

123 White Elephant

Medium Screen print on textured paper

Brief Illustration inspired by The White Stripes' album
'Elephant'. The image reflects the bands minimalist
approach and bold sound

AOI **membership** benefits

The Association of Illustrators provides a voice for professional illustrators and by force of numbers and expertise is able to enforce the rights of freelance illustrators at every stage of their careers.

Membership of the AOI is open to all illustrators, illustration students, agents, lecturers and illustration clients.

All categories of membership receive the following benefits:
- Free distribution of The Journal
  – The Essential Illustration Magazine
- Discounted rate for Images – competition entries, hanging fees and annual pages
- Contact details on AOI database for enquiries from clients
- Discounts from many material suppliers
- Discounts on AOI events and publications.

In addition, we provide the following services for particular types of membership:

Full Membership
This category is for professional illustrators who have had a minimum of three works commissioned in the previous 12 months prior to application and accept the AOI code of conduct.
- Legal advice on contracts
- Information on pricing and professional practice
- More than 50% off on one-to-one portfolio surgery
- Business advice – an hour's free consultation with a chartered accountant on accounts, book-keeping, National Insurance, VAT and tax
- Full members are entitled to use the affix 'Mem AOI'
- Reduced rates on online ImageFile.

Associate Membership
The benefits are the same as those for full membership but this one-year category is for newcomers and illustrators on their first year out of college who have not yet published work. In exceptional circumstances this membership can be extended by an extra year.

Student Membership
This service is for students on full-time illustration or related courses.
- One-to-one advice on entering the profession
- More than 50% off on one-to-one portfolio surgery
- Further discounts on AOI events, publications and competition entry

Corporate Membership
This service is for agents and clients from the illustration industry who adhere to the AOI code of conduct.
Further benefits:
- Free copy of the Images illustration annual
- All corporate members' staff and illustrators will receive discounts on events, Images and AOI publications

College Membership
College membership entitles the college to the following benefits:
- Large discounts on AOI events and publications
- Link to college web page from AOI site
- Free copy of the Images illustration annual
- The right to use the AOI member logo on publicity

Additional options (at extra cost) include:
- Portfolio consultations
- Career Advice lecture, covering self-promotion, copyright, pricing, licencing, the work of the AOI, and the speaker's working practice etc.
- Discount on bulk orders of additional copies of the bi-monthly Journal, Rights & Survive
- Degree show presence on AOI website

For an application form and cost details please contact:
Association of Illustrators
2nd Floor, Back Building
London EC2A 3AR

Tel: +44 (0) 20 7613 4328
Fax: +44 (0) 20 7613 4417

E-mail: info@theaoi.com
Website: www.theAOI.com

AOI Publications

Survive

The Illustrator's Guide to a Professional Career
Published by the AOI and revised in 2001, *Survive* is the only comprehensive and in-depth guide to illustration as a professional career. Established illustrators, agents, clients and a range of other professionals have contributed to this fourth edition. Each area of the profession, including portfolio presentation, self-promotion and copyright issues, are looked at in detail. The wealth of information in *Survive* makes it absolutely indispensable to the newcomer and also has much to offer the more experienced illustrator.

Rights

The Illustrator's Guide to Professional Practice
Rights is an all inclusive guide to aspects of the law specifically related to illustration. It includes information about copyright, contracts, book publishing agreements, agency agreements, how to seek legal advice, how to calculate fees and guidance on how to write a licence.
Rights is the result of a number of years research. It has been approved by solicitors and contains the most detailed and accurate model terms and conditions available for use by illustrators or clients.

The Troubleshooting Guide

A handbook written by solicitors Ruth Gladwin and Robert Lands (Finers Stephens Innocent) covering essential legal issues surrounding subjects such as animation, collage, web-sites, and advice about taking cases to the small claims court.

Report on Illustration Fees and Standards of Pricing

The AOI have recently published a report entitled 'Illustration Fees and Standards of Pricing'. This publication is compiled from existing AOI data, general survey results and contributions from agents, art buyers and selected working professionals. Research suggests that the decline of fees and/or commissions charges for illustrations in recent years has resulted in many business failures. Properly researched costing and pricing structures is a central plank in maintaining business viability. Illustrators should consider the true cost of their services when determining rates. AOI hopes that this report will encourage both illustrators and commissioners to create awareness of the importance of carefully considered pricing.

Client Directories

The Publishing Directory lists ca. 180 and the Editorial Directory more than 300 illustration clients with full contact details; the Advertising Directory holds details of over 200 advertising agencies who commission illustration – providing an invaluable source of information for all practitioners. Each directory includes notes of what kind of illustration is published by the client and we update and add contact details to each list every year.

The AOI Journal

The Essential Illustration Magazine

The AOI Journal, re-launched in Summer 2000, covers a wide range of issues related to the illustration industry including:
• current industry affairs
• illustration events
• reviews
• interviews
• letters
Regular contributors include practitioners, educators and industry professionals. The Journal provides a forum for on-going debate, and a valuable insight into contemporary illustration.

Published six times a year. Free to members.

Ordering Publications

To order publications or subscribe to the Journal, please send a cheque, made payable to the Association of Illustrators, clearly stating your contact details and which publications you would like to purchase to:

AOI Publications
2nd Floor, Back Building
150 Curtain Road
London
EC2A 3AR

For payment by Visa, Mastercard or Maestro, please call
+44 (0)20 7613 4328
or subscribe/order online:
www.theaoi.com/publications.html

www.**theAOI**.com   www.**AOIimages**.com

Evolving year on year, theAOI.com is the definitive resource for UK illustrators. The site is comprised of five main sections:

AOI Information Centre
- Regularly updated news, events, links and listings sections.
- Documents, including Acceptance of Commission form, AOI Report on Illustration Fees and Standards of Pricing 2005, Guide to Commissioning and more.
- Articles. Fully searchable archive of texts drawn predominantly from the AOI's Journal publication.
- Other sections include full information about AOI membership, Publications, Submissions, Personnel and latest Press Releases.

ImageFile
The ImageFile is a keyword searchable illustration collection in two parts.
- Permanent Collection: features published works categorised by industry usage.
- Portfolios: Artist-maintained portfolios, featuring up to twenty works by each illustrator. Provides the facility to upload images, delete, edit caption info and more, from the convenience of their own computer.

Images Book
Recent Images annuals, in their entirety, online and searchable.

Directory
The Directory provides direct links to the work of illustrators whether on their own site or within their agent's or other corporate site. Now linking to the work of over 1000 illustrators.

Discussion Board
A moderated discussion board open for all to read and post. After registering, users can reply to existing messages or start new topics.
The Board has five forums including Professional Practice, AOI Feedback, Tools of the Trade, General and Classifieds.

Launched in 2003, AOIimages.com was specifically developed as a client entry point to promote illustration to the creative industries. It features specially tailored information pages plus the Permanent Collection, Portfolios, Directory and Images Book sections as outlined above.

About the illustrators

A Agent
T Telephone
F Fax
M Mobile
E Email
W Website

To call from outside
the UK add the prefix '44'
and omit the first '0' from
the number provided

Index of **illustrators**

About the illustrators

A Agent
T Telephone
F Fax
M Mobile
E Email
W Website

To call from outside
the UK add the prefix '44'
and omit the first '0' from
the number provided

Darren Hopes   204
A Début Art
30 Tottenham Street
London W1T 4RJ
T 020 7636 1064
F 020 7580 7017
E debutart@coningsbygallery.
demon.co.uk
W www.debutart.com

Peter Horridge   47
Maribonne
Bunbury Lane
Bunbury, Tarporley
Cheshire CW6 9QS
T 01829 261 801
F 01829 261 801
M 07775 583 760
E peter@horridge.com
W www.horridge.com

Sandra Howgate   228
Flat 7, Rendlesham House
Rendlesham Road
London E5 8PB
T 020 8986 0532
M 07729 529 530
E info@sandrahowgate.com
W www.sandrahowgate.com

Frazer Hudson   76, 242
354 Manchester Road
Crosspool, Sheffield
South Yorkshire S10 5DQ
T 0114 268 2861
M 07973 616 054
E frazer@dircon.co.uk
W www.frazer.dircon.co.uk

Rian Hughes   212
2 Blake Mews
Kew TW9 3QA
T 020 8896 0626
F 020 8439 9080
M 07979 602 272
E rianhughes@aol.com
W www.rianhughes.com

Rod Hunt   95
63 Ashburnham Place
Greenwich,
London SE10 8UG
T 020 8469 0472
M 07931 588 750
E rod@rodhunt.com
W www.rodhunt.com

Stefan Isaacson   252
41 Bannerman Street
Liverpool,
Merseyside L7 6JP
M 07719 940 265
E stefanisaacson@hotmail.com
W www.stefanisaacson.co.uk

Giulio Iurissevich   198
A Début Art
30 Tottenham Street
London W1T 4RJ
T 020 7636 1064
F 020 7580 7017
E debutart@coningsbygallery.
demon.co.uk
W www.debutart.com

Adrian Johnson   12, 13, 86
3rd Floor
67 Farrington Road
London EC1M 3JB
T 020 7430 0722
M 07958 670 750
E mail@adrianjohnson.org.uk
W www.adrianjohnson.org.uk
A Central Illustration Agency
36 Wellington Street
London WC2E 7BD
T 020 7240 8925
F 020 7836 1177
E info@centralillustration.com
W www.centralillustration.com

Matthew Johnson   67
110 Rounton Road
Bow, London E3 4EX
T 020 7987 6711
M 07941 516 449
E matthewjohnson@hotmail.com
W www.matthewjohnson.me.uk

Wendy Jones   218
The Art Department
46 Edge Street
Northern Quarter
Manchester M4 1HN
T 0161 835 3343
M 07949 005 251
E wendy@the-art-dept.co.uk
W www.wendyjones-artist.com

Sophie Joyce   237
18 Rochester Street
Brighton
East Sussex BN2 0EJ
T 01273 888 231
M 07855 764 413
E info@sophiejoyce.com
W www.sophiejoyce.com

Satoshi Kambayashi   49, 90, 91
Flat 2
40 Tisbury Road
Hove,
East Sussex BN3 3BA
T 01273 771 539
F 01273 771 539
M 07739 179 107
E satoshi.k@virgin.net
W www.satillus.com

Per José Karlén   38
Flat 2, 309a Uxbridge Road
Acton,
London W3 9QU
M UK: 00 44 (0)7944 087 361
E per.karlen@perpictures.com
W www.perpictures.com

Paul Keysell   220
1 Elsinore
Warwick Court
Stratford-upon-Avon
Warwickshire CV37 6YN
T 01789 415 676
F 01789 415 676
M 07780 605 178
E paul@paulkeysell.com
W www.paulkeysell.com

Mary Kilvert   178
The Old Corner House
Broad Street, Weobley
Herefordshire HR4 8SA
M 07813 182 020
E marykilvert@hotmail.com

Bev Knowlden   234
2 Priory Terrace
Totnes,
Devon TQ9 5QE
T 0870 162 0611
M 07941 035 708
E bev@bevsdecorum.com
W www.bevsdecorum.com

Olivier Kugler   142
A The Artworks
70 Rosaline Road
London SW6 7QT
T 020 7610 1801
F 020 7610 1811
E steph@theartworksinc.com
W www.theartworksinc.com

Delphine Lebourgeois   176
38 Fieldhouse Road
London SW12 0HJ
T 020 8673 3164
M 07963 057 769
E dlebourgeois1@aol.com

Matt Lee   57
33 Sherbrooke Road
Fulham
London SW6 7QJ
T 020 7610 1585
M 07759 984 669
E mail@matt-lee.com
W www.matt-lee.com
A Eye Candy Illustration Agency
Pepperpot Corner, Manor Yard
Blithbury Road, Hamstall Ridware
Staffordshire WS15 3RS
T 020 8291 0729
E mark.wilson@eyecandy.co.uk
W www.eyecandy.co.uk

Yvonne Lee   158
Clock Cottage
5 The Green, Weston on Trent
Derby DE72 2BJ
T 01332 690 399
M 07837 729 984
E yvonneplee@hotmail.com

Richard Levesley   241
94 Coltsfoot Green
Luton, Bedfordshire LU4 0XT
T 01582 668 258
M 07729 532 324
E r.levesley@btinternet.com
W www.jprwhite.co.uk/richard
A The Art Market
51 Oxford Drive
London SE1 2FB
T 020 7407 8111
E info@artmarketillustration.com
W www.artmarketillustration.com

Henning Löhlein   108, 109
Centre Space
6 Leonard Lane
Bristol BS1 1EA
T 0117 929 9077
F 0117 929 9077
M 07711 285 202
E henning@lohlein.com
W www.lohlein.com

Frank Love   84
the dairy studios
5-7 Marischal Road
London SE13 5LE
T 020 8297 2212
F 020 8297 1680
M 07930 492 471
E thedairy@btclick.com
W www.thedairystudios.co.uk
A Eastwing
99 Chase Side
Enfield EN2 6NL
T 020 8367 6760
F 020 8367 6730
E andrea@eastwing.co.uk
W www.eastwing.co.uk

David Lucas   133
The Drawing Room
Panther House
38 Mount Pleasant
London WC1X 0AN
M 07941 716 888
E dav.lucas@virgin.net

David Lynch   185
9 Godrer Twr
Llaingoch
Holyhead
Anglesey LL65 1BQ
Wales
T 01407 763 813
E info@david-l-lynch.com
W www.david-l-lynch.com

Patrick MacAllister   192, 193
23 Vicars Oak Road
London SE19 1HE
T 020 8761 5578
F 020 8761 5578
E patrick.hat@talk21.com

Ric Machin   115, 197
A Début Art
30 Tottenham Street
London W1T 4RJ
T 020 7636 1064
F 020 7580 7017
E debutart@coningsbygallery.
demon.co.uk
W www.debutart.com

Peter Malone   125
A The Artworks
70 Rosaline Road
London SW6 7QT
T 020 7610 1801
F 020 7610 1811
E lucy@theartworksinc.com
W www.theartworksinc.com

James Marsh   87
8 Cannongate Road
Hythe
Kent CT21 5PX
T 01303 263 118
M 07973 114 019
E james@james-marsh.co.uk
W www.jamesmarsh.com

Mick Marston   191
107 Montgomery Road
Nether Edge
Sheffield S7 1LP
T 0114 281 8440
M 07799 487 795
E mikiluv@blueyonder.co.uk
W www.mikiluv.com
A Central Illustration Agency
36 Wellington Street
London WC2E 7BD
T 020 7240 8925
F 020 7836 1177
E info@centralillustration.com
W www.centralillustration.com

Daren Mason   192
Morden Holt
4c Priory Way, Datchet
Berkshire SL3 9JQ
T 01753 544 290
F 01753 544 290
M 07710 769 203
E daren@squarecurve.com
W www.squarecurve.com

Index of **illustrators**

About the illustrators

A Agent
T Telephone
F Fax
M Mobile
E Email
W Website

To call from outside
the UK add the prefix '44'
and omit the first '0' from
the number provided

Index of **illustrators**

About the illustrators

A Agent
T Telephone
F Fax
M Mobile
E Email
W Website

To call from outside
the UK add the prefix '44'
and omit the first '0' from
the number provided

AOI **Portfolios**

Now in their second successful year, AOI Portfolios have been designed for illustrators to have access to their own, easily-maintained, online presence. Subscribers can benefit from increased exposure to the traffic attracted to *theAOI.com* and *AOImages.com* websites, averaging some 1500 daily visitors in 2004.

The main features of AOI Portfolios include:

- Simple, easy to use, password-protected facility allowing illustrators to manage their own online portfolio.
- Upload, replace or edit up to 20 portfolio images - any time, and from any computer connected to the internet.
- Automatic resizing of main (large) images.
- Automatic creation of thumbnails!
- Animators - feature your own Flash or Quicktime movies!
- Portfolio introduction includes presentation icon, contact information and links to your email and homepage.
- Individual image captioning. Headings include your own/agents contact details, image description, client list and biographical information.
- Domain name option allowing clients direct access to your portfolio.
- Free addition to the AOI Directory with listing linking to your portfolio.

Complete information including submission form and schedule of fees can be found at:
http://www.theaoi.com/portfolios

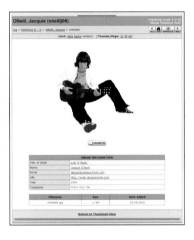

Corel® Painter™ IX - the world's most powerful Natural-Media® painting and illustration software is NOW AVAILABLE and it's better than ever!

.... But don't just take our word for it!

'With its improved performance, brush handling, filter effects, path snapping and new artist oils, Corel Painter IX keeps its creative crown.'

PC Pro Magazine, Issue 122

'Painter is one of those apps that, no matter how long you use it, continues to amaze at every turn. Buy it now. You won't regret it.'

Computer Arts Magazine

'Painter's strength remains in its realistic simulation of artistic effects and brushes. It is still THE application for digital artist.'

Digital Creative Arts Magazine

Corel Painter enables some of the world's most accomplished creative professionals including commercial designers, artists and photographers to extend their natural talents and techniques to create original works of breathtaking digital art.

Increased Performance and Productivity
Brush Control Palettes provide easy access to all brush settings and controls.
Improved Speed 'turbo-charged' brushes average two times faster. Some brushes are 10 times faster.

Creativity
Artists' Oils Painting System - apply paint blends created in the Mixer palette.
Snap-to-Path Painting - create perfect vector-path brush strokes or shapes. Save time particularly when creating illustrations or conceptual sketches of mechanical objects such as cars or aeroplanes.
Quick Clone speeds up the image - cloning workflow and reduces five steps to one.
Digital Watercolour - Significant enhancements mean that paint stays wet between sessions, allowing you to start one session where the last one ended.